PRAISE FOR *STAYING AFLOAT*

"*Staying Afloat* is a worthy successor to Cash's previous memoir, *Tortilla Chronicles.* It is far more than personal reminiscences, but an intimate history written in a delightfully unpretentious style."

—Lucy R. Lippard, author of *Pueblo Chico: Land and Lives in Galisteo Since 1814.*

"A fearless confession of the twists and turns in the life of a singular artist and treasured storyteller."

—Raúl Garza, Media Consultant

"Cash's writing in *Staying Afloat* is a compelling and enjoyable read; an engaging narrative set in Santa Fe with rich descriptions and a warm inviting ambiance that transports the reader through several decades of her challenging life experiences."

—Guadalupe Goler, Santa Fe icon and author of *Just 4 Kicks.*

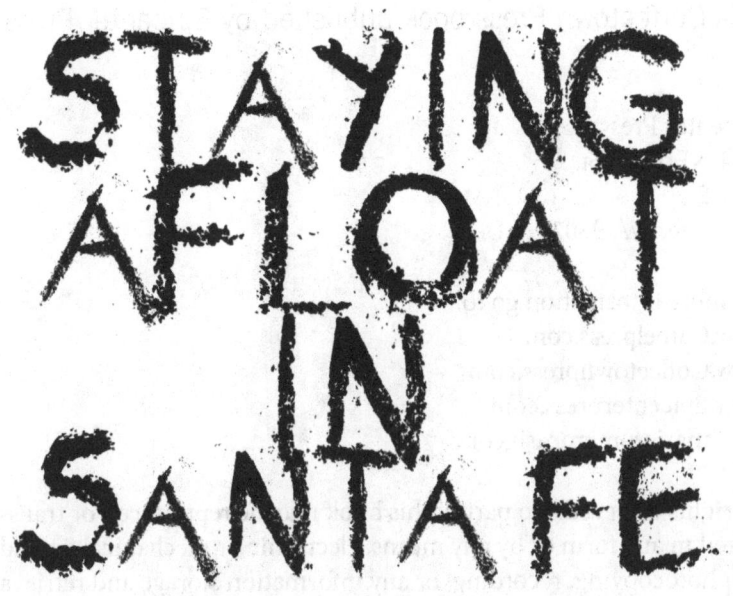

STAYING AFLOAT IN SANTA FE

AN ARTIST'S JOURNEY

MARIE ROMERO CASH

coffeetownpress

Kenmore, WA

coffeetownpress

A Coffeetown Press book published by Epicenter Press

Epicenter Press
6524 NE 181st St.
Suite 2
Kenmore, WA 98028

For more information go to:
www.Camelpress.com
www.Coffeetownpress.com
www.Epicenterpress.com
www.marieromerocash.com

This is a work of fiction. Names, characters, places, brands, media, and incidents are either the product of the author's imagination or are used fictitiously.

Cover design by Scott Book
Design by Melissa Vail Coffman

Staying Afloat in Santa Fe

Library of Congress Control Number: 2023945718

ISBN: 978-1-68492-165-2 (Trade Paper)
ISBN: 978-1-68492-166-9 (eBook)

This book is dedicated to family and friends,
those gone and those still present, who always encouraged
my journey as an artist and writer.

ACKNOWLEDGMENTS

Everything in life begins and ends with family. I am grateful that whether visibly present or not, you are present in every moment of my life and every page of this memoir. Although it took me forever to finalize this book, I am grateful to Jennifer McCord and Coffeetown Press for their willingness to bring it to life.

Everyone has a past.
Everyone has a future.
It's the part in between that can boggle the mind.

—Marie Romero Cash, 2023

PROLOGUE

After the publication of Tortilla Chronicles (a memoir about growing up in Santa Fe during the 1950s) I had not planned to write a sequel. All these years later, I realized I had been writing such for more than twenty years and the time had come to finish it. There was no specific urgency, but I hoped my story would give other women insight into their own lives. We've all heard the quote, *when life gives you lemons, make lemonade.* Since I never seemed to have enough sugar, it took me these many years to gather all those lemons into the same basket.

This story is not primarily about relationships. It is about what happens when an individual unknowingly lacks the skills to maneuver through everything that life throws in their direction. We come into this world a blank slate, and through adequate attention, nurturing and time, the road is paved toward success. Without it, the primary focus becomes staying afloat long enough to swim to shore.

—Marie Romero Cash, 2023

1 | FILLING IN THE BLANKS

SINCE MY BIRTH IN 1942, I have lived in Santa Fe, New Mexico, surrounded in the spring by purple lilacs and in the fall by bright buttercup yellow chamisa bushes, loved for their color, despised as an allergen; among piñon trees which every September shed their sticky cones bursting with pine nuts; and flat-roofed adobe houses with bright red chile strings hanging from a nail on their front porches. The jagged peaks of the Sangre de Cristo Mountain range are visible from my front window. I am fortunate to live where skies are such a deep hue of blue that artists are challenged and eager to duplicate.

This desert town experiences all four seasons. Although much to my chagrin during winter, a thick white blanket of shimmering snow covers the mountains like vanilla frosting on a sheet cake. I am not a winter person, preferring spring and fall, period. Yes, I understand the need for sufficient water to see the city through the summer months, and I'm sure it's not very PC of me, but it is my preference. I attribute this snow-hate to having spent many winter mornings walking two or more long miles to St. Francis Catholic School in downtown Santa Fe with snow up to my knee-caps. (Eyeballs will roll on this one, but remember, at that age I was likely only a bit over three feet tall.)

I adore my furry black dog, a Border Collie/Lab mix named Milly. I wish she could speak and tell me why she breaks into moments of sheer abandon, spinning in circles while she scatters dust throughout the yard, then rolling in the dirt and weeds until she flops to the ground in delight. I would also like to know what she is thinking or seeing as her ears perk up when there's nothing in sight, and why in winter she prefers to lie in a snowbank rather than on a comfy cushion in front of a warm fire.

A decade ago, back on the cold January morning of my seventieth birthday, I awoke to the sound of birds chirping noisily outside my bedroom window. Just what the heck time was it anyway, that these feathered creatures found it necessary to jar me loose from a peaceful slumber? I pulled the down comforter over my head hoping to return to dreamland, but to no avail. Once awake, no matter the time, I'm up for the duration, irrespective of the amount of sleep I managed to garner. Milly has her own internal clock, and it rarely jives with mine. What had I been dreaming about, anyway? Maybe one of those guy-gets-girl-and-they-ride-off-into-the-sunset-and-live-happily-ever-after dreams. That would not be unusual since I've always considered myself a dreamer (and an optimist), hoping a new love is just around the corner.

I momentarily considered a seventieth birthday to be monumental and that I should do something special; then I decided to stay in bed. Along with the onset of that day came the unsettling realization that most of my life was now behind me, and I wasn't sure I was ready to greet a day which could very well herald events I wasn't prepared to face. There were seven of us in our family. One of my brothers passed away at sixty-four and then I wondered if that was the cut-off age for the rest of us. I don't think I'm over the anger of God taking him. Another brother passed from cancer in 2010, at seventy-three; followed by a sister and the two remaining brothers, all blows to my existence. Usually, death is not an event easily processed, unless it's your own, and then there's not much you can say about it.

Eighty-one years on God's green earth! Whoever coined the phrase *time flies* hit the nail on the head. My inner diva was only about fifty, and my inner child had been reborn in the previous twenty years and was still struggling to stand upright. There was no disputing the fact that I'd spent most of my life just trying to keep my head above water; to stay afloat long enough to get my bearings so I could swim ashore to safety.

I have never paid much attention to the aging process. The wrinkles must have appeared overnight, because suddenly they were more visible. Oh, I'm not talking about any deep furrows where you could plant flowers or hide a camel, but small, subtle lines (not unlike celebrity author Nora Ephron's book, "I Feel Bad About My Neck") that reflected I might have been around the block a couple of times. Vanity was not one of my weak points—I was what I was—a smidge over five feet, curly fly-away, once-blazing auburn red hair, hazel eyes and an ongoing struggle to lose the extra fifteen pounds that seemed to hold on for dear life. For many years, my interior furnace was fueled by comfort food—hot steaming bowls of *posole* with red chile, warm tortillas with butter, and other foods from my childhood. A psychologist might conjecture that I was feeding my loneliness.

So why was I lonely and what was I longing for? I was surrounded by family and friends. Most of my basic needs were being met, albeit in a struggling economy. (My car was paid for and I still enjoyed driving around Santa Fe, having learned as a teen by revving up my father's 1949 Ford and driving it up and down the gravel driveway until I felt secure enough to pull it out onto the street. Like most cars of that era, it was equipped with a clutch and a stick shift; no automatic trannys or power steering. In junior high driver training, we were pounded with the rules of the road, and today I can still parallel park like a pro and I'm happy to report I've gone through my entire life with nary a traffic ticket.)

Could it be that I was craving attention; that I felt my soul withering away and had no idea how to retrieve it? It would be frivolous to apply to each individual everything that has been written about children of alcoholics. There are degrees of alcoholism just as there are degrees of its effects. A sponge can absorb twice its weight, and a soul surrounded by imaginary walls can deflect only as much as necessary to survive at any particular moment. There are cubicles and compartments in my brain populated by as many unpleasant events that I could cram in there without having to address them. Among them are the reasons I traveled through life completely oblivious to the smell of roses.

I'm sure most young girls entertained fantasies about being rescued from her family life by a knight in shining armor astride a magnificent white horse. He would swoop them up and carry them away to a life of bliss and wonderment. In my case, we would reside in an adobe castle somewhere among the piñon and junipers, where we would live happily ever after. One might wonder what became of those fantasies. I imagine they still exist, embedded somewhere in the shadows of my mind waiting to be resurrected or dismissed; rearranging the clutter to make room for bigger and better things, particularly that one huge thing—life. Yeah, life just got in the way of my dreams and fantasies. Nothing turned out the way I had imagined it. John Lennon had the right idea: *Life is what happens when you're making other plans.* But I didn't have a plan. I was winging it.

2 | FAMILY MATTERS

I WAS RAISED IN A SPANISH-SPEAKING HOUSEHOLD in Santa Fe. My ancestors hailed from Spain by way of Mexico, and we considered ourselves Spanish-American, not the more recently coined *Hispanic* term which tossed an umbrella over all off-white American citizens not branded with other labels. I was born on West Houghton Street, a small neighborhood in the South Capitol area of the city. It was a neighborhood of primarily Spanish-speaking families, dirt roads, streetlights shot out by BB guns, and outdoor bathrooms. In recent years I lived around the corner from West Houghton Street, and after I sold that house, I now rent a small adobe directly behind the house where I was born. I have come full circle, returning to the neighborhood of my childhood, where the apricot tree my father planted in 1930 leans its branches over the wall in my back yard and provides magnificent shade on sunny days and an overabundance of juicy fruit.

My father, Emilio Romero, a tall, light-complexioned man, was born in 1910 into an old Santa Fe family whose roots stretched back to 18th century New Mexico. They were people of ordinary means, but proud. He attended the old brick Catholic school on Guadalupe Street until the eighth grade, which for that era was equivalent to a high school education. Since as a young man he was the breadwinner for his family, hawking newspapers on a downtown corner no matter what job he took he taught himself everything he needed to know to get by. He was a hard-worker willing to take any job. After he married, he worked for the U.S. Forest Service, and installed fencing around many of the mountain ranges in the Pecos Wilderness around Santa Fe. During that period he transported and planted the gigantic blue spruce trees which still stand against the north wall of St. Francis Cathedral and almost reach the height of the church.

My mother, Senaida, a small woman with dark hair and hazel eyes, was also descended from early Spaniards. On the other hand, she had only a sixth-grade education and was fortunate to have that. She was by no means illiterate and could read and write both languages. She attended classes in a small two-room school in the community of *Ojo de La Vaca* (Cow Springs) until she was eleven. There were no grade distinctions then, as all children attended the same school regardless of age and learned from the only teacher in the village.

In that isolated village on Rowe Mesa northeast of Santa Fe, her family endured harsh winter storms with seven-foot snowdrifts which kept them cooped up indoors for weeks at a time. They had relocated from Santa Fe to that remote area when the U.S. Government handed out parcels of land to individuals through the Homestead Act. Like her four siblings, she was born at home, the birth assisted by a midwife and probably on the wooden kitchen table which had been sanitized and covered with sheets and towels.

Once a month a physician from Santa Fe traveled to the village to examine a wide array of inhabitants, from the newborn to the elderly. His black bag was filled with the magic drugs of the era, aspirin and sulfa, a few homeopathic remedies, and not much else. The 1918 influenza epidemic devastated the village, eradicating entire families. My mother's family survived, but after her father succumbed to throat cancer or some other undiagnosed ailment, the family returned to Santa Fe. A few years later, she met my father.

In 1930, my father built a two-bedroom house from thousands of hand-made adobe bricks on land he had purchased across from his parents' home on West Houghton Street. By all standards ours was a simple house with a small kitchen and two bedrooms, one of which served as a living room. Every room had wooden *vigas* on the ceiling and wood floors. There were two concrete steps at the entrance to the shady porch in front of the house. It too was of adobe construction, and in my mind that porch could have been made into an additional bedroom, since some of my siblings slept out there in the cool summer nights. Much later I would discover that in Santa Fe a porch was a symbol of prestige, and every house in that neighborhood had one. The front yard was bordered by an adobe wall and filled with apricot and apple trees, lilac bushes, and irises of every color.

The house had been newly plastered in the late 1930s, but within a few years the plaster began to separate away from the walls, giving the exterior a worn and dilapidated appearance. There were outdoor bathroom facilities for the seven children and two adults living in our home until the 1950s when my father added a large kitchen and bathroom. We would no longer have to bathe in a metal tub in a corner of the kitchen. The outhouse was situated on the edge of the driveway between houses and was shared with the relatives next door. Before the introduction of packaged toilet tissue, I'm told there was always a Montgomery Ward's catalog in most of the outhouses in the area, a fact I personally don't recall.

My father would be employed as a sheet metal worker for Zia Company in Los Alamos until he retired. As a teenager in 1925, my mother worked for the Santa Fe Electric Laundry. When she married and became a full-time housewife and mother, that would be all she ever knew. From 1930 on, one of my siblings was born every two years and after my birth in 1942, she had a six-year respite until the last of my brothers was born in 1948.

My parents were ordinary individuals born shortly after the turn of the twentieth century. They didn't talk much about how they met, nor that my mother became pregnant when she was twenty-one and he twenty. There was never a word about how she broke the news to him or how he might have reacted to the news. In fact, it wasn't until after both had passed that my sister Rosalie and I discovered an odd bit of information. We were going through some old papers and ran into their marriage certificate, something my mother had kept well hidden from prying eyes all those years. From this time-worn yellowed paper, we learned that their wedding had taken place six months prior to their first child's birth. The ceremony was conducted by a justice of the peace and not a priest, which was unusual for Catholics at the time.

There was never any record that they had later repeated their vows in a church, but they remained devout Catholics their entire lives. Since they never seemed to celebrate anniversaries, I wonder now if they might have been ashamed that they were forced to get married. *Forced* might be too strong a word, but it fits. Based on my father's upbringing, he would have had little choice but to do the *right thing*, and that would have been to get married, whether he was willing or not. My grandmother, Anastasia Rodriguez Romero, would not have expected any less of him. Everything else aside, they were together for fifty-seven years, until death they did part, and he never once forgot her July 18th birthday. It was not yet apparent to me that my mother possessed great inner strength to endure that many years with one man, particularly this one.

I grew up watching my mother canning peaches, plums and apricots in Mason jars stacked neatly in the cupboard. She was industrious and yet fully aware of what it had been like to be hungry as a child. My siblings and I really knew nothing about hunger, not like she had experienced. Many of her family meals consisted of weak broth made from boiled bones thickened with flour and seasoning. She once said she hated to eat fish in any form because it was the food which made up so many of their meals to keep them from going hungry. Fishing in the nearby Pecos River was one of the ways her father provided food for the table. Tortillas and beans were a staple at most of our meals, accompanied by generous helpings of red or green chile. Store-bought bread and jam were foreign to us until a small grocery store at the corner of our street opened for business in the 1950s and we were able to experience these, in addition to packaged candy, frozen pops, and sugary baked goods.

My mother prepared meals from scratch, even in hard times. In the midst of labor union strikes and layoffs, we never went hungry. Non-staple foods were unknown to us. We ate chicken, venison, goat, lamb, beef, and maybe rabbit thrown in for good measure. Oatmeal and Cream-of-Wheat or eggs were the usual breakfast fare, and a brown-bag sack lunch eaten at school consisted of some foodstuff slammed between a tortilla and wrapped in waxed paper, which we hurried to assemble each morning before we left for school. These we devoured in an area far from where other students ate their more appealing lunches.

My parents were simple folk, more concerned with daily survival than politics, world affairs or the ups and downs of the stock market. In a third world country, they would be considered commoners such as those raised in small villages in the first quarter of 20th century America. Interaction between them consisted of the usual husband/wife mother/father daily life banter about feeding a large family on a limited income during times of economic hardship throughout the country. We were too young to comprehend what went on in their lives and in their heads. Mealtimes were determined by my father's work schedule. He departed for work each morning before seven and returned home before five that afternoon. By the time he sat down to have a few beers and read the local newspaper, the table was set before him. No matter what, we always gathered for the dinner meal. That was an unspoken rule. There were few discussions about world events. Conversation was kept at a minimum, so as not to disrupt his mood.

Sometimes when things were off kilter, my father turned to alcohol, and life careened into the canyons of dysfunction. Our floors were literally paved with eggshells, which we tiptoed around, hoping to not call attention to ourselves or reveal some infraction we had committed, no matter how insignificant. I was too young to determine if my father was a true alcoholic or even be aware that the Spanish word, *boracho,* meant drunkard. As an adult I would decide my father fit the profile of a binge drinker, who only wiped out once every few months by drinking steadily for two solid weeks and then recovering for two or more additional weeks. This was repeated at least once a year . . . twice if the planets were out of alignment. I detested his drinking. I was torn between loving and hating him. He would fall from the pedestal on which I had placed him many times during my childhood and continue into adulthood and long after. I never wished him dead, but I worked hard at wishing him sober. It was exhausting and I was disappointed that my wish never came true.

It seemed that my powers as a magician had not been properly cultivated. I was an abject failure. To paraphrase a 21st century aphorism, *what happens in Las Vegas stays in Las Vegas,* and this was certainly true in our household. The entire emotional trauma caused by my father's alcoholism was sealed in like a pressure cooker. There was no place to hide but out in the open. We practiced invisibility, overlooking tirades and emotional outbursts. We developed turtle-thick skin, and words slid off our backs like butter, and what happened at home, stayed at home.

The dynamics of drinking aside, when I was eight years old I was under the impression that swimming was like walking—it came naturally. Not so. A freak series of events would alter that belief. I almost drowned in a private pool on Old Santa Fe Trail, and if my cousin Gilbert hadn't pulled me up, a tragedy would have occurred. It is no wonder that I would spend the rest of my life trying to stay afloat long enough to swim ashore.

3 | LIFE IN THE SLOW LANE

I'M NOT SURE EXACTLY AT WHAT POINT I began to spend most of my days leading an imaginary life. I don't recall any childhood trauma that would have initiated the need to begin constructing walls which would shield me from anything unpleasant. Like most children my age, I was required to live at home, but as far as I knew, there was no statute of limitations to living inside your brain, where it was safe and dark. The constant tension experienced during my father's drinking bouts was difficult, to say the least, but my sister and I kept ourselves busy with mundane household tasks or homework. The boys in the family could spend their non-school hours away from home, without valid reason or permission.

As is a common trait of children of alcoholics, I subconsciously chose dual roles: the comedian and the one who could be relied on to fix things. I was a sweet, smiling people pleaser. I would do or say whatever it took to make my father laugh and by doing so divert the attention and tension away from my mother and anyone else in the family. He was not visibly violent toward her, but during those times he often had a vile mouth which could cut through her like a knife. Outwardly, she seemed to not be affected by his tirades, but I knew that deep down there was an impact comparable to a bowling ball colliding with the headpin.

I'm certain my continuous antics endeared me to my father, as my siblings always referred to me as his *favorite.* (Years later, a psychiatrist would inquire: *His favorite what?* I perceived this to be an odd question. Just what was she trying to read into my childhood? I had not been physically abused, molested, or locked in a closet.) My other self-assigned childhood role, that of little Miss Fix-it often came into play. I could take care of things, make arrangements, fix something, and I was good at it. I was always in ready mode—ready to run, ready to eat, and ready to go into action if my father wasn't home by sunset on Friday, assuring my mother that everything was fine, that he had a flat tire or had to work late, or any other excuse I could pull out of the air. Of course, she knew better. That role followed me into adulthood, as I was often summoned to take care of something that required my expertise.

I don't believe I was fearful of my father, but I was afraid of what might happen if he ever became really angry. Even though rumors were whispered at the clothesline and kept hush-hush of local men who beat their wives in a drunken rage, we still listened with wide eyes, assuring ourselves it would never happen at our house. I was never able to drift into slumber until I heard my father's car come up the driveway, and I slept with one eye open until I assured myself that he had fallen asleep.

If it sounds like we had a terrible childhood, I can honestly say it wasn't all that bad. As siblings growing up in the fifties, I would venture a guess that we led parallel lives with other young people across the country. We went fishing and rock hounding, conquering mountains like Sun Mount to the east of us to view the entire city from above; using a Geiger counter at Tent Rocks near Cochiti Pueblo looking for outcroppings of uranium; we skated on borrowed or stolen skates; played marbles and jacks on the hard ground and enjoyed treats such as popsicles and popcorn balls. We watched our parents and neighbors struggle through the hard times, but yet they danced joyously at baptisms and weddings where the strains of violins and guitars, accompanied by an accordion and an off-key singer, filled the air with joy and laughter.

4 | LOVE, THE FORMIDABLE FORCE

At some point in her life, my mother had turned to prayer. Was that all she had left; had she exhausted all her efforts and emotions? Did she suddenly realize that love was not the answer unless it was reciprocal? She was a loving, simple woman, with only a minimal education to maneuver her through life. The prayer and novena book she used for over sixty years is today worn and tattered. On almost every dog-eared page there are faded pencil notations where she kept track of the days remaining for each nine-day series of prayers. Each evening when the house was quiet and the kitchen was tidied, she sat at the head of the table, her novena book open to a page marked with a time-worn pink silk ribbon. The sound of her glass rosary beads clicking against the table in continuous rhythm was memorable.

My mother prayed to every saint in her book for each of us and probably to a handful of other saints when her prayers went unanswered. Saint Jude, the patron saint of the impossible, appears to have been the saint she turned to most often. She was determined that her faith would see everyone through. Included in her ritual were prayers for the dearly departed, relatives, friends and neighbors, and for the ill and infirm. There was no end to the dialogue she had with the occupants beyond the gates of Heaven, who, according to my father, listened to every request she dialed in.

As a family, we were an odd bunch. A psychoanalyst would likely venture an opinion that we were a byproduct of a dysfunctional family, a term nonexistent in the 1950s. We had no idea how to survive our own lives, let alone join in on the journey with another person. Historically, women fall in love imbued with hope and determination for molding that potential mate into the man of their dreams. Men of that era looked for someone like their mothers, who would take care of their needs, bear their children, cook and clean, and not complain. Based on this belief system, each one of my siblings would eventually enter into problematic marriages and short-term relationships, most of which were destined to dissolve into thin air.

In recent years, because of readily available DNA testing, individuals have surfaced out of the woodwork who claim to be the offspring of my older brothers, long after their passing. These online results seemed to match me up as an aunt to a string of previously-unknown nieces and nephews, who had been put up for adoption early in their lives. Each of them was looking to connect to their birth parents, and I was the one available missing link. It is sad that they were never able to know the men who had fathered them.

In her memoir, Nora Ephron wrote that she lived through an era when nobody was divorced. As an adult, I was living through an era where everyone around me was divorced. Despite the stigma attached to separation or divorce, at the time it seemed to be the only way out for many. Like lemmings, we continued to climb the cliff only to find the mistake was repeated more than once. With any luck, the realization might appear that there had to be something wrong—with me, with them, with everyone. Five out of seven of my siblings had multiple divorces. My eldest sister Anita was the first in the family to tread that thin line, but she remarried quickly and stayed in that relationship for half a century. She was followed by brothers Bobby, Jimmy, and Ricardo. Emilio and Rosalie survived unscathed, and I topped the charts with a lifetime record of four. As Jerry Lee Lewis would say, there was a whole lot of shaking going on.

I had always dreamed of love. Of being in love. Of being loved. My father came home with our first television set in 1950, a ten- or twelve-inch Motorola with metal rabbit ears, that probably set him back a month's salary. As often as I could, I sat in the living room and watched half-hour programs that were then considered sitcoms and which I believed depicted reality. The viewing options were sponsored by well-known providers such as Colgate and Maytag, i.e., one sponsor for the entire program as opposed to today's ten minutes of commercials for twenty minutes of viewing. Before television, I sat at the kitchen table with my mother each day listening to radio novellas such as *The Romance of Helen Trent*, which ran for over seven thousand episodes, along with *Our Gal Sunday*. How could they have depicted any form of reality since words such as pregnancy, infidelity and divorce were not allowed by the networks. It was all about love and unrequited love, and everything always ended up happily ever after.

From birth on, little girls are primed to fix their radar on finding Mr. Right. Their love antennae hone in on any male who offers even a modicum of attention. They are provided dolls at an early age to teach them to nurture a love for babies and motherhood. Once the prey is bagged and a relationship begins to develop, we are giddy with happiness until immortal bliss begins to fade like the evening star on an overcast night. The notion of love was all in our heads. With every relationship, we wanted it to be ever-present and that resulted in becoming desperate and crazy when it wasn't. So, the search resumed.

I have forgotten many things about my childhood. I wonder if we ever laughed hysterically about some inane event that had no explanation in real time. Were there occasions when we arrived home after school, anticipating hugs and smiles from our parents in a house filled with love and laughter? Did we look forward to dinner as a family, talking with our mouths full about the great day we had and the fun things we did at school? Or did we just sit there on the worn yellow vinyl and chrome chairs, hearts stuck in our throats, waiting for the other shoe to drop?

Before my seventeenth birthday, I had the dubious distinction of never having been kissed. In those days, female offspring of Spanish families in our neighborhood were rarely allowed to attend social events without supervision—not like our Spanish Colonial ancestors who left the upbringing of young girls to spinster-nanny types whose main task was to preserve the chastity and well-being of their wards; but more on the level of strict rules which precluded young women from being out of the house after sundown.

Oh, but evident as the imaginary imprisonment was, I still had hope. This was not an unusual situation for 1950s good girls. After all, most of my cousins residing nearby lived under the same set of standards similar cultures adhered to. Being lured into engaging in anything beyond puppy love and awkward attempts at romance was prohibited for obvious of reasons. First of all, my all-encompassing fantasy world did not include the tools to cope with the dose of reality that anything beyond that might very well bring as a consequence, i.e., teen pregnancy, unwed mother, fill in the blanks. It was far safer to embellish the fantasy with quick pecks on the cheek or neck, holding hands and looking into the eyes of that handsome knight, while quickly brushing away any advances attempted by determined and daring teenaged hands. Besides, I knew not of what I speak, having yet to experience anything even closely resembling *like*, let alone *love*.

5 | THE KNIGHT APPEARS

It was a hopeful inevitability that the opportunity to date someone who was not imaginary would come around, even for someone as blighted as I considered myself to be. I was besieged with self-doubt and found it hard to believe that at last, I had been *chosen*. I would no longer sit on the sidelines, watching as couples paired up and walked around the school grounds holding hands and interacting with other couples on their way to have a soda at Free Fraser Pharmacy on College Street (now Old Santa Fe Trail) or the soda fountain downtown in the Plaza square.

I experienced all the bubbly feelings I associated with being in love. It didn't matter that my own feelings were not factored into the equation; all that seemed to be of importance was that *someone, anyone,* was interested in *me,* and that was enough for the moment. I glommed on to the opportunity to be half of a duo, one of two, part of a couple, hoping to spend as much time away from home as I could get away with, even if I had to lie about it.

Teenage girls without boyfriends populated a separate and distinct group from girls with boyfriends, and, imaginary status or not, I had been part of that disparate section of young womanhood for a long time. We weren't allowed to wear makeup, but after school before we entered the house, both my sister and I vigorously wiped any trace of lipstick from our lips.

This particular Prince Charming was three years my senior, not particularly handsome, and by today's standards probably a six. I was his second girlfriend ever, and I suspected his mother preferred family friend Rhoda to me, as her name was mentioned often enough in casual conversations. When we met, he was in his junior year of high school, with few apparent aspirations of making it to graduation. This attitude was fueled by the notion that he could find a job with the N.M. Highway Department because his father was employed there. Being a high school drop-out wasn't well received by most parents, but hey, I had a boyfriend and his potential for moving from prince to pauper was a hurdle I hadn't yet addressed.

Tall and lanky, he was clean-cut, blue-eyed and friendly-faced, with wavy slicked back brown hair. He had a Roman nose with a pronounced bump in the middle. Of Italian/Anglo descent, his mother was only thirty-four years old, and his father was ten years her senior. The Italian grandparents spoke sparse English, but were enthusiastic and sociable, she with a crooked old finger which pointed to Heaven whenever her daughter-in-law poured herself another shot of vodka, and he with sky blue eyes that peered through Coke-bottle lenses. They were both under five feet tall and reminded me of salt and pepper shakers. The entire family lived in a Territorial style red brick house with high ceilings on Manhattan Avenue, three blocks from the downtown plaza. Every Sunday the smells of simmering Bolognese sauce wafted from the open windows out onto the street.

I was no stranger to observing people as they drank. Like most families, including mine, my new boyfriend's family had its secrets. Theirs were stashed in the many liquor bottles his mother hid in the pockets of at least a dozen coats and jackets in the bedroom closet. Ours were the endless nights kept awake by a father who insisted that someone get up and pour him a drink, even though the whiskey bottle sat on the headboard within his reach.

Life in the 1950s was very complex. It was never *Modern Family* or *The Brady Bunch,* but rather *La Familia meets the Twilight Zone.* My father ruled with an iron hand; my mother was much more understanding and sighed visibly each time he insisted on adherence to his rules. My sisters and I were not allowed to wear shorts or halter tops during our teen years, and this carried over to our lives as adults. Yet when a scantily clad woman walked across the downtown park, the heads of all the men in a hundred-foot radius, including my father, turned a full 360 degrees.

My closest sister and I rarely attended school dances or sporting events because our curfew was ten o'clock. Our father did not feel compelled to give us an explanation for anything, suffice it to say it was enough that if he said so, that's all there was to it. He was also over six feet tall and strong as an ox, and we were not about to entertain meaningless confrontational opinions questioning the reasons why we weren't allowed to do something. No matter how we felt, respect still ran deep. That didn't keep us from lying for each other just to get out of the house. In 1958 during my sister's senior prom, which she had been invited to attend by the young man she would eventually marry, I pretended it was also my prom night, and dressed in a formal gown, complete with corsage and all. My boyfriend and I went to a movie at the Yucca Drive-In, and I was home by eleven with fabricated stories the next day about what a fun time the dance had been. I would often wonder if my sister was going to keep our secret, since she had also seen me smoking near the bathroom window one night and had nothing to lose if I did something to annoy her.

My mother knew very little about sex education, more than likely having learned by trial and error. She did what had been expected of herself, her mother, and grandmother. There was little information on the subject in upper levels of education. We heard about *rubbers* but had no idea what they were and couldn't even imagine their purpose. No condom and banana demonstrations conducted by the nurse to hoots of all the males in the classroom. We were not taken aside to have *the talk*, and whatever information we gleaned about sex came from snippets of conversation overheard in bathrooms and lockers or from more worldly fellow students. I'm sure my parents were aware that men were sexual beings, so they knew what to expect. We didn't, and nobody bothered to enlighten us, but we knew darned well it was a situation we had to avoid.

My father was less than thrilled at the prospect of his daughters dating. Even though we didn't catch the nuance, he intimated to my mother that when we got married, we would lose our childlike qualities and a virtual stranger would be responsible for us, not someone of their choice. My brothers could date whomever they pleased, but the girls were a different story. Our oldest sister couldn't wait to leave home and at seventeen was gone with the wind. Every bit as stubborn as my father, he was powerless to forbid her from leaving. With or without his blessing, she was moving to Albuquerque, a nearby utopia with two military bases and nightlife that went on far later than that in Santa Fe. In 1949 at nineteen, Anita was chosen Santa Fe fiesta queen and a year or so later married an airman stationed at the Air Force base in Albuquerque. After that, I think my father would have preferred my remaining sister and I become spinsters, wear our hair in a bun, not shave our legs or armpits, and live at home for the rest of our lives.

6 | PREPPING FOR THE FUTURE

On graduation night in 1959, I became engaged. I had recently turned seventeen, and although there was no reason to accept his proposal, I must have felt something inside me that this might not ever happen again, so I feigned enthusiasm and jumped at the chance. There was an obvious expression of disdain and disappointment on my father's face as we shyly made our joint announcement and displayed the ring with the miniscule diamond prior to entering the gymnasium for my class graduation ceremony. We planned to be married the following year. If my father would have had his way, he would have grabbed me by the shoulders to shake some sense into me.

The 1950s concluded with a wonderful promise of things to come. I continued to be starry-eyed and hopeful, without a clue about what adulthood or marriage entailed, in anticipation of the wedded bliss which would occur within a year. Along with the two hundred graduates from Santa Fe High I started looking for employment. Jobs were scarce for my age group, but I scored one with the First National Bank as a junior clerk, near the bottom on the pay scale but adequate for my needs. After all, this would be my first actual paycheck. Imagine all the cool things I could buy. The worst thing I did that year convinced me I wasn't cut out for it. Because of my lack of training by a secretary more interested in lunch with her coworkers, I mistakenly transferred $100,000 instead of $10,000 to a client's account, and it took the bank's officers the rest of the afternoon to work the kinks out of that transaction. My face glowed with embarrassment, so I spent the remainder of the day sitting on a settee in the downstairs lounge.

Months later I found a job with a small law firm, a more challenging career and a monthly salary of $100. I reported for work on the first Saturday in August, which was also the day of my Grandmother Anastasia's funeral. Fearing I would be fired before I even started, I hoped she would understand why I wasn't there to see her off to her final resting place.

The small and stuffy offices were on the second floor of an old building in the middle of downtown above what is now the Plaza Café. (The memory of the place is so vivid that I have used this same office as the setting for the protagonist in my published series of Jemimah Hodge mysteries.) The windows were the only ventilation and when they remained open, all the street sounds from below could be heard, incessant horn honking by teens circling the plaza in their souped-up cars coupled with the odor of tail pipe exhaust fumes. The rooms smelled musty, of old books and papers, and the wood floors creaked noisily. The main secretary was scheduled for maternity leave, and she spent a minimal number of hours familiarizing me with the ropes. Too often after that I heard a litany of praise for her from the partners, and I suspected I would not be able to fill her immense shoes.

With no experience in an office setting, I should have paid more attention in Mrs. Kegel's shorthand class during my senior year. I walked into the attorney's office with an air of efficiency, and sat down in an old leather chair, steno pad in hand and pencils sharpened. My boss was around fifty and semi-bald and had deep blue eyes with huge bags under them. He didn't appear to be very friendly, or perhaps I wasn't used to such professional demeanor. He had a dismissive air and explained nothing as he began to rapidly dictate a long legal document. Not only was the terminology all Greek to me, but I had difficulty keeping up. I only caught every other word and thought I could fill in the blanks later. Wrong.

I managed to pull together about six double-spaced legal-sized pages with four carbon copies. (This was shortly before IBM Selectric typewriters were introduced where errors could be easily lifted off by pressing a backspace key, or a computer keyboard with a delete button. Here, if you made a typo, you had to neatly erase the original and the four copies as well.) I paper-clipped the completed documents to the file and placed them on his desk. It wasn't long before he summoned me into his office. He was red-faced and flustered, and said he was astounded that the final document read nothing like the one he had dictated. I sat meekly with my hands in my lap and admitted he was going too fast for me to keep up and I thought I could fill the words in. Truth was, everything he said was unfamiliar terminology. He retorted that I could have said something, but I'm not sure that was true. He then re-dictated the entire thing at a much slower pace. I was able to retype it before I went home at seven that evening.

As the sun began to set, I walked the two miles from the downtown plaza south on Galisteo Street to my neighborhood, past fragrant lilac bushes hanging over long adobe walls. To top off a miserable day, stories of *La Llorona* filled my head as I walked. This was the legendary bogeywoman from a popular folk story in New Mexico who crouched behind trees and walls waiting to pounce out and scare the bejesus out of someone whose bad demeanor had gone asunder. My assumption was that this included more than naughty children, as how could she differentiate. And added to my dismay, on that street there was a particularly intimidating character along that way whose actions and mannerisms frightened most children, let alone adults.

Since I was afraid of the dark and also nearsighted, I squinted my eyes and scoured the street before me for bogey people while

I filed away my feelings of embarrassment, fear, inadequacy and anxiety in the designated compartments of my brain. I had just experienced another of life's survival lessons, and I wasn't sure I could take another one. I thought this job had been a big mistake and wondered if I would ever be able to make it through. *Why did we have to grow up and be adults, anyway*?

7 | THERE WENT THE BRIDE

SO, HAVING SURVIVED CHILDHOOD without too much apparent damage, I proceeded to enter into an engagement to be married. As was the custom in both Spanish and Italian families, our parents met for a (shorter than usual) discussion, and since both families were Catholic, a church wedding was inevitable.

The previous year, my sister had married her high-school sweetheart, and her beautiful bridal gown waited in a box in the bedroom closet for me to wear. Albeit a hand-me-down, it was the perfect dress for the perfect wedding. It had a high collar with long sleeves, a Chantilly lace bodice and an A-line skirt. A pair of size six white linen pumps purchased at JCPenney would complete the outfit nicely. (After the ceremony, the dress and veil would be donated to the Carmelite Monastery on Old Pecos Trail where it would be used by novitiates becoming nuns.)

That June day took an eternity to arrive, and as we gathered at the church, the first thing to go wrong was that the best man, my brother Emilio, had left the rings on top of the washing machine at my parents' home. I remember throwing a fit about how irresponsible he was, but I knew that was just a cover for my true emotions which were about to boil over as we stood behind the last pews near the entrance to the church waiting for him to make the twenty-minute round trip in his 1955 Studebaker.

Standing there with the members of the small wedding party, I was plagued with the realization that I was about to make a horrible mistake. I didn't want to get married. I had no concept of what it would entail, and I wasn't eager to find out. I wanted to bolt out of the church screaming at the top of my lungs that I couldn't do this. I should have walked away, but I didn't have the courage. That fateful day, relatives, guests and parishioners dressed in their Sunday finery had already taken their seats. Had I not known better, I would have thought it was someone else's wedding. I could see all the way down the aisle, fragrant flowers attached to the front pews of the church, the priest checking his watch. I do not even recall what flowers my bridal bouquet consisted of, and if there was a maid of honor and flower girl.

The church seemed deafeningly quiet, but my mind was about to explode. Why was I here . . . was it too late to walk away? Would my parents ever forgive me if I did? All I could think about was the humiliation they certainly would endure. I imagined they would be the target of vicious finger pointing and gossip and we would never be able to live the shame down. I now wonder where these thoughts of humiliation came from. I never considered my town to be *Peyton Place*. I was overwhelmed with sorrow and sadness. I could have put the brakes on all this a long time before it got to this point. I was in love with the prospect of being in love. There was music in the air, delight in children's voices. But I was only there in spirit.

My brother rushed in with the rings. The musicians began to play the Wedding March and the priest motioned for us to come forward. Those fifty footsteps were the longest walk I have ever taken in my life. Even today, the whole ceremony in the church and the later reception are a complete blur. An event which should have been one of happiness is so deeply buried in my mind that I wouldn't be able to retrieve it even if I tried.

I didn't want to remember that day anyway. I had no idea what the word *commitment* meant, or its ramifications in a Catholic wedding. I was stuck in playing the role of a happily engaged young woman about to fulfill her dream of marriage to the man of her dreams and the happily ever after that was supposed to follow. I was eighteen going on twelve. Standing at the altar, I turned to look across the pews at my parents, wanting to run to them, pleading for them to forgive me for lying that this was what I wanted, for pretending I was even capable of making a decision of this magnitude. But I didn't. Truth was that the true definition of love had not yet emerged. I was a little girl playing a grown-up game, completely oblivious to the long-term consequences.

I stood at the altar with my heart racing and prayed for the church to be demolished by an earthquake or a thunderous bolt of lightning. That didn't happen either, so the ceremony dragged on. I imagine it was followed by a reception at some fraternal hall, where music played and the guests danced and drank, but that too is part of the memories deleted by the crash of my interior computer.

The fairy tale was falling apart at an alarming rate. In my fantasy-filled state of mind, I had imagined the honeymoon would be as dreamy as the wedding should have been. Today, if someone suggested my in-laws would be driving us to our honeymoon destination, I'd think they were crazy. That's exactly what happened.

8 | THE HONEYMOONERS

My betrothed had a wealthy aunt who resided about two hundred miles from Santa Fe. The day following the wedding, along with a trunkful of suitcases, the four of us were packed into the coral and black '57 Chevy Bel Air for the trip. As we drove along the highway, we played a game where each time a Volkswagen Beetle came into sight, we hollered out *slug bug*! and punched the person of our choice in the arm. The one who counted the most peenie-weenie VWs won the game. That's how immature I was. The maturity level of everyone else in the car should have also been apparent.

In 1961, the town of Farmington, New Mexico was a one-newspaper town with a population less than that of Santa Fe at 30,000. A strong odor resulting from oil and gas explorations in the vicinity permeated the area along the highway, but to me it stunk in more ways than one. I was Marie Antoinette headed for the matrimonial guillotine, not having a clue as to what to expect.

We arrived at the residence of Aunt whatever-her-name-was. The house, for the times, was a large modern home with a pitched roof and a two-car garage. We were greeted by the couple at an entry area the size of a small bathroom. The expansive living room was furnished with ornate wood furniture, with puffy velvet cushions on the couches, and a matching lounge chair and ottoman in front of the television set. An ashtray sat on every table and the liquor cabinet in the corner was bulging with bottles. It was definitely different than my parents' house, and trashiquely more opulent than my new in-laws' home.

Dinner was, of course, something Italian, with lots of spicy marinara sauce over meat having simmered for hours in a roasting pan in the oven. We sat around the dining room table as though we had all been invited just to have dinner and then spend the night. I felt awkward and afraid; of what I didn't know, but I suspected it was the events which would follow lights-out after schmoozing in the living room was concluded. In the back of my mind, I knew this was not a marriage that was going to be consummated if I could help it. How naïve was I that I thought the evening was going to be different; had I not even considered that I would be expected to put out once I signed the marriage certificate; that things were going to be much different than sitting at the drive-in, necking and petting? I might have been in a state of shock, because looming around the corner it appeared that the subject was about to be approached.

Later that evening after conversation had waned and fake yawns emerged in its place, we were casually directed to the master bedroom, and more subtly to its oversized four-poster wooden bed with an overstuffed mattress. The bed was made up in a style I envisioned one in a hotel would be, with purple satin pillows and matching sheets and comforter. *Imagine,* this couple had given up their comfortable bed for their nephew to consummate his marriage, and they were sequestered in one of the spare bedrooms (I surmised) to listen for the sounds of the night. The sounds they probably heard were me throwing up in the bathroom. *I was not going to do this, no way, no how.* In hindsight, I realize I never considered his reactions of surprise and disappointment, if that's what he was feeling since he did not have the opportunity to defile this particular flower.

The next morning, I sat in front of the large oval mirror on Auntie no-name's old-fashioned dressing table with a smaller magnified electrified makeup mirror on the side. Fascinated by all the different shades of lipstick, makeup and eye shadow, I sat entranced. Since I wore little makeup, I had only seen such an array at the downtown Woolworth store and had never owned but one tube of lipstick at a time. I adjusted the slant of the mirror and dabbed a bit of peacock blue eye shadow on my eyelid and leaned forward to survey the results. I followed with an application of mascara and a swirl of hot pink lipstick.

We went downstairs for breakfast, another major cooking affair. I ignored the subtle winks and glances traded between the adults as they passed the tray of waffles, sausage and eggs around the table. If they were expecting a play-by-play of the night's events, they weren't going to get it from me. I was a no-show at that ball game. To my embarrassment, though, my hostess did take notice that only one of my eyes was made up and took the opportunity to mention that it was a common practice to do both eyes when making up one's face. Her offhand remark elicited gales of laughter from them and an embarrassing exit to the downstairs powder room for me.

Through all the inane small talk and snide winking, I wanted to disappear into the woodwork. Breakfast sat like a lead ball in my stomach. Had I driven there alone, I would have bolted for the door and been on my way. Instead, I smiled meekly and thanked them for their hospitality and mumbled the usual hollow good-byes and hope-to-see-you-agains. I tried to appear happy and energetic as I took my place in the back seat next to my obviously dejected husband.

9 | THE LONG JOURNEY HOME

I DON'T RECALL HAVING HAD MUCH TO SAY on that midday trip back to Santa Fe. It seemed many more hours longer than the drive to get there. We dropped his parents off and proceeded to the small one-bedroom apartment we had rented on Allendale Street, a block from my parents' home and three blocks from his. To say I was beyond miserable would be making light of the situation. I would have preferred to erase the previous week from my life and still be living at home with my family. Believe me, my father's sternness and the once resented house rules would have been welcome at that point. What the hell kind of fairy tale was this, anyway?

For months we continued to play house, both of us working during the day. An opportunity came up to purchase a home in the new Bellamah housing district a few miles south, just off Cerrillos Road, and we proceeded to qualify with a down payment loan from my brother-in-law. Owning a house at a young age was a big deal at the time, and it managed to skyrocket our debt level as we bought all the furnishings on credit. We were already stretched out as far as we could be, and I was still an emotional wreck over continuing to play at being married, or more definitively, at being an adult.

The reality was that from the beginning the marriage was destined to crash and burn, and a year or so later it inevitably did just that. Someone had forgotten to send me the happy marriage manual. There were a number of reasons, the main one being our sex life, or lack of it. When we were finally intimate several months following the honeymoon, I'm pretty sure it was forced. Yes, I now understand the frustration he must have felt, but then I felt as though I had been violated (and perhaps had been). I had no feelings for him or for myself. The later result of that experience would serve to catapult me into a secret, indiscriminate affair with the office manager of the firm where I worked, and later with an art teacher from Montana, as I subconsciously decided to renew and continue the search for the elusive knight. I shudder to think that I never considered what consequences could have resulted from either of these liaisons.

I no longer had aspirations of a future in the marriage. We weren't ever going to iron out the problems I perceived to be insurmountable. I spared my family any details of the floundering relationship. Eventually I'm sure they thought I'd lost my mind, even though they didn't verbally express it. I could sense it through their body language each time I walked through their kitchen door. When my attorney had the divorce papers served, my husband never knew what hit him as I prepared to walk out of his life, never to look him in the face again. (All these years later I have had moments where I realized he deserved an explanation, but I had no idea what I would have said, then or now, and the opportunity never arose.)

I made the decision to divorce on my own, not feeling the need to discuss it with anyone, including him. I was brought up believing divorce was unacceptable in my culture and religion. There was an underlying stigma attached to a woman who chose to leave the comforts of home and move on. It was a silent condemnation, not a subject discussed by friends and family over morning coffee. I entered into divorce just as I entered into marriage—clueless. There were debts to share, furnishings to divide and memories to stuff in a crevice somewhere. I kept the house and the mortgage that went along with it; he kept the red 1963 Ford he had thrown us into debt over, thinking I would be impressed by a shiny new object, and it would somehow serve to save the marriage. Unfortunately, there was no saving something that hadn't been worth saving from the beginning. For the rest of my life, I didn't even count this as a marriage, and I blotted it out from my mind.

I went against the grain of everything that had been pounded into me since childhood: *Women needed a man to take care of them, to provide all their needs and put a roof over their heads. It was a woman's duty to take care of her man, bear children, keep the house clean and be an available sexual partner.* I was one acorn that did not fall close to the tree.

10 | EXIT STRATEGY

WHILE I WAITED FOR THE FINAL DECREE to be issued in the divorce, I began a job with the Bureau of Indian Affairs. An *avant-garde* (for the times) art institute in Santa Fe had recently opened on the campus of the existing 1940s Indian School on Cerrillos Road. (The term *Native American* did not come into use until the civil rights movements later that decade.) Indian students from all over the United States and Alaska travelled to Santa Fe to begin or continue their education at IAIA and also learn the basics of Indian art or to improve on their already inherent talents. Because of their affiliation with this innovative art school and their own undeniable talents, instructors such as Alan Houser, Charles Loloma and Fritz Scholder would go on to become internationally known artists.

I was hired as secretary to the assistant director of the Art Department. At twenty-one, I was still young, naïve and impressionable, and particularly enjoyed interacting with the art teachers and students, both of whom could be highly eccentric. At my previous jobs I was accustomed to stuffy employers who wore suits and ties and expressed little interest in knowing me as a person. For the most part at the Institute, with the exception of the upper-level staff of directors and secretaries, the casual attire bordered on

Bohemian. Eccentric personalities like those of clothing designer and art director Lloyd Kiva New and jeweler Charles Loloma, although foreign to me, were fascinating.

I had not been aware of having a particular interest in art, other than arts and crafts pursued in elementary school and on my own as a teenager which included experimenting with copper enameling and other crafty projects. At the Institute, there were three female instructors who taught ceramics, weaving and photography. Along with the male instructors, each of them exhibited a unique unorthodoxy, and staff meetings were never concluded without mild reprimands from Dr. Boyce, the Director of the Institute, for those who strayed from established protocol.

The instructors were all serious artists, not all experienced in teaching situations, but were aware of the task they had been handed, that of molding these young individuals into artists. They often gathered together as comrades, and were all participating in a grand experiment, which in time would either succeed or fail. In my own life, the need for artistic expression would not surface until decades later, and the stimulation provided by my experience at this institute would remain dormant for that same period.

Within days of the start of the semester, students trickled in from Idaho, New York, Florida, Arizona, Alaska and other points in the United States. For many of them, it was not only their first time in an airplane, but also the first time they would be away from home and family. It was less stressful for others who were driven in from Indian pueblos within a seventy-mile radius of Santa Fe. At the time, every student was a ward of the Federal government, with the BIA being responsible not only for their education, but for their safety and well-being as well. They were not allowed to leave campus for any reason unless it was a school-sponsored event. Their medical needs were taken care of at the Public Health Service hospital and clinic adjacent to the campus. There were therapists available for any emotional needs which might come about due to separation from family or immersion into a multi-cultural situation. For many, their interaction with "white people" had been minimal up to that point. There were also historical factors to consider, i.e., long-standing feuds between tribes such as the Navajo and Hopi.

I noticed that student couples paired off quickly, and many formed small cliques, either with students from their tribal or state affiliation. Many were past high school age, and some lacked the self-confidence and sophistication necessary to survive alone. Family and cultural rituals were of great importance to most and those were not included in their daily schedules. At the time, I was closer to the students' ages and easily formed friendships, although the directors frowned on this practice. As part of the divorce settlement, I had retained the residence a few miles southeast of the campus, so although prohibited, thought little of having a small group of students dropping by nights and weekends to eat pizza and watch TV in my living room. Since I did not drink alcohol, Cokes and 7UP were the only beverages in my refrigerator and I would have thought twice about ever providing alcoholic beverages to minors. As I gravitated toward these new young friends, I wondered why the Spanish culture did not have a school to cultivate our artistic talents.

After a year of interacting with students on a regular basis at school and sometimes hanging out with them in the evenings, I found myself drawn to a nineteen-year-old Hopi student from Arizona who sat close by as we all watched TV and ate pizza at my house. During the day as he passed by my office, he would stick his head in the door and say hello. His best friend was from Sitka, Alaska, where the only way in and out of the village was by seaplane, and the two kept me in stitches with their tales of life on their respective reservations. Both were equally shy, but friendly and open in my company.

As uncertain as I was about love and what it entailed, I began to experience all the school-girlish emotions when we were together. Maybe it was puppy-love fun, or was it serious? I had no real way of knowing. I had already developed the ability to put into play whatever spin was necessary at any given time. After all, how else could a girl live out her fantasy? Perhaps I had not matured much in the previous year and was ready to again venture into the unknown. Nine months later, we both decided to leave the school and move to California. I do not recall what prompted us to come up with this decision. Maybe it was because of the rules against dating a student, so our relationship was kept secret, or it was based on immaturity and sheer stupidity. Plan A was that I would transfer to the BIA in Sacramento, and he would also find a job there. Just like in the movies, everything would work itself out. Jobs equaled money, housing, food and fun. I would soon discover later that we didn't have a Plan B.

To get the ball rolling on this potential pipe dream, I tendered my six weeks' notice, and the week before we were to depart, he gave his notice to the registrar. A number of his fellow students and faculty were aware of our plan. Charles Loloma, the Hopi jeweler who would rise to international fame within a few years, and his wife Otellie, a potter whose works had been featured at the Chicago Art Institute, both gave us parting gifts. His were silver and gold wedding rings, and hers were small, incised clay wedding pots. Their assumption that we were headed into marriage preceded ours. Alan Houser expressed his distaste for the situation by wagging a long Apache finger at me, his frown unaccompanied by words to express whatever he was thinking.

11 | BEST LAID PLANS

I COLLECTED MY FINAL PAYCHECK, and we took off in a 1959 Pontiac that months before I had managed to buy on credit, having been rendered carless by the divorce. As we drove south on Cerrillos Road onto the highway toward Albuquerque, droplets of rain battered the windshield as I watched the lights of Santa Fe disappear in the rear-view mirror. The adventure was on. In the back of my mind, I wasn't completely sold on the idea of leaving home for the first time in my life, but I wanted to be with the knight, no matter what it involved. With my vast experience of telling fairy tales, I had concocted a story for my parents about going to California for a few months to work on a project with the female photography instructor from the school. I'm not sure they bought the story, but I didn't give them time to protest.

With the exception of the fateful honeymoon trip, it would be the first time in my life I had traveled more than sixty-five miles away from home for any reason. That night we stayed in Gallup at a nondescript motel off the highway. We registered with his first name and my last, for no apparent reason. It could have been that subconsciously we were fearful of being discovered and sent home like two naughty runaways. Neither of us had any idea of where this relationship was heading. The next day as we slowly wound our way out of New Mexico and into Arizona and then California, I realized the obvious: we hadn't thought this whole thing through. Being with someone full-time was a lot different than spending a few stolen hours together during the week.

The assumption that my job transfer to Sacramento would be approved might very well become a reality. The BIA had processed my transfer request and there was a strong possibility I qualified for a secretarial job; but neither of us had researched the cost of living or anything else connected to life in a new city. (Since he was the knight, I was relying on him to have all the answers, not realizing then that some young knights are not very worldly or wise.) The three-year difference in our ages was beginning to look more like ten.

We arrived in Sacramento the day before my scheduled interview. I contacted the personnel office and was placed on hold for an inordinate length of time and shuffled to several departments where I was repeatedly requested to continue to hold. Finally, a woman came on the line and asked where I was staying, was I traveling alone, and where could I be reached. She also asked a few questions that I thought were irrelevant, as I did not yet have answers. I told her at that time I didn't know where I would be staying, but I would call the next day and let her know, after which I promptly hung up.

That evening I called home to let my parents know the imaginary teacher and I had arrived safely in California. My mother informed me that an FBI agent had contacted them the previous evening, inquiring if they had a son named B and how he could be contacted. I continued to lie to them that I was traveling with the art instructor and had no idea what they were talking about. I doubt if they were naïve enough to believe the inconsistencies in my story; after all, my divorce had taken them by surprise, and I still owed them an explanation for that one. I told my mother not to worry and assured her I would call once we settled in and began the "project."

There was no doubt in my mind that something was amiss. I didn't bother to call the BIA office to follow up on the interview, suspecting that there might be more trouble in the wind than it was worth. We decided to spend another night and then drive to Arizona. We repacked our suitcases, tossed them into the Pontiac and headed out. That afternoon we traveled down Interstate 5 and took a quick tour of Carmel by the Sea. I had never been this close to an ocean. It took my breath away, but not in a good way. Noisy whitecaps pounded against jagged dark rocks, in my mind an ominous setting for an ocean named Pacific. There was nothing pacifying or peaceful about it.

Following our poorly planned trip to Sacramento, we had about three hundred dollars between us. I would discover some months later that if the FBI had caught up with us, I would have been in big trouble for transporting a minor across state lines, particularly one who was a ward of the Bureau of Indian Affairs. That would have been more devastating for my parents than had I walked away from my wedding. Today, with all the technological advances in tracking, we would never have even made it to the Arizona state line.

12 | DESERT STORM

As we motored across the arid countryside, the air was hot and dry, unlike the lush green landscape of California from where we had departed the previous day. Even with all the windows down, the heat was unbearable. I was acclimatized to the coolness of Santa Fe, a 7000-foot altitude surrounded by the jagged snow-peaks of the Sangre de Cristo Mountain Range, and the area we were in was as foreign to me as the Gobi Desert. At any moment I expected to see a herd of camels crossing the highway or a mirage of a water hole surrounded by palm trees off in the distance.

The AM radio station fluctuated between slow jazz and static, and we had long run out of small talk. Noticing the silent mood the knight had slipped into, I was apprehensive about asking too many questions, but assumed we were on our way to his parents' home on the Colorado River Indian Reservation. I was nervous about meeting them. In the seemingly endless quietude, I checked the map often to see how we would get there, and which exit we would take, since we were on the only highway leading to the turnoff. To my surprise, when we were within thirty miles of the town, he drove past the exit and continued in silence until we reached the outskirts of Phoenix, where we stopped at a Whataburger stand in Wickenburg to sate our mutual thirst and hunger.

Although he didn't say so, it hadn't occurred to me that his parents were probably unaware of his untimely departure from the school, and he might not have been ready to face the inevitable backlash in case they had been contacted by school officials. I also now imagine that the FBI had also been in touch with them and we would have been apprehended as we drove down the graveled road leading to their house.

An hour later, we arrived in Phoenix. What an immense metropolis this was compared to my miniscule hometown of Santa Fe. The city was spread over a vast expanse of flatland, peppered with gigantic Saguaro cacti with spiny arms outstretched to the sky. For being a desert, everything was verdant, wrapped in blankets of lush plants and grass. Multi-storied buildings reached into the skyscape, each competing with the other for air space.

We scoured the local newspapers and within a few days we found a reasonably-priced small studio apartment on the northwest side of the city and then both ventured out to look for jobs. He scored one at a nearby hospital, and I landed one in a downtown law firm. Six months zoomed by and between our two paychecks, we eked out an adequate survival. Although we had never discussed marriage, in my mind I'm sure I was working toward an eventual *us,* some sort of permanent arrangement. I wasn't even remotely aware of what *his* mind was working toward. At some point, I came to the realization we were just biding our time, but I did my best to ignore that.

My concept of survival revolved around togetherness. I was a long way from home and had no friends or family to reach out to. Another month or so passed and I noticed he was spending more hours away than his work schedule required. We had only one vehicle between us and it occurred to me that whenever I picked him up after work, there was an attractive carrot-headed girl hovering in the general vicinity. They worked in the same section of the hospital, preparing food trays twice a day to be distributed to patients.

As I rolled into the parking lot one afternoon, I saw them leaning against a wall, deep in conversation. I swear they were holding hands. I parked and made my way over to introduce myself. She said it was nice to meet B's sister. In a split second it became apparent to me that if there had been any obvious clues that he was interested in seeing other women, I had overlooked them. I felt pangs of jealousy and betrayal and fired questions at him on the way home. He would only say that I was making something out of nothing, but my insecurities began to swell. I started to wonder if I should have stayed in Santa Fe and again was feeling much older than the few years that separated us.

13 | FAMILY PLANNING 101

As a teenager I suffered severe and debilitating monthly cramping, and a family physician told my mother it was likely I would never be able to bear children because of a tipped uterus. (Then a fact, now an urban legend.) Consequently, I was not concerned about becoming pregnant, figuring it was just as well. From the horror stories related by my mother and other women as they discussed their experiences, I had mixed feelings about childbirth. None of them ever indicated it was an easy process but likened it to expelling a ten-pound watermelon. How fortunate that I had avoided pregnancy in that first marriage or any subsequent liaisons because of the stranglehold it would have held on my life.

Besides, at this point in time my track record with men hadn't been that impressive, what with one divorce under my belt. I had been regular as a clock with my 'monthlies', but at that time I was feeling anxious about why my usual discomfort hadn't yet arrived. A quick trip to Walgreen's and a positive pregnancy test an hour later confirmed my dreaded suspicions. My hands were shaking as I repeated the process twice, praying that the initial test was defective. It wasn't. So, there I was. Twenty-three years old, living in sin and now pregnant. I had broken all the rules pounded into me both at home and in church. I wasn't sure what the average male's reaction might be when receiving news that his live-in girlfriend was expecting their child, but a month after I revealed the news. I got my answer.

It was 1965 and tribal offices all over the southwest had received notice that young men enrolled through their tribe were potentially in line to be drafted for the war in Vietnam. In order to choose the branch of service they would prefer to serve in, it was highly recommended they should trot themselves down to the enlistment office and sign up immediately. A quick wave goodbye at the airport and he was gone by August.

Were the events leading up to this sudden necessary enlistment in the Air Force a trumped-up story? I'm not sure and I didn't question it then, but eight weeks would pass before I would hear from him. I fluctuated between thinking I had been abandoned and would surely end up having and raising a child by myself and believing I would hear from him at any moment. I checked the mailbox every day, only to find it empty. Basic training in whatever state he was in was apparently someplace where communication with the outer world was forbidden. I was still naïve enough to believe that, and I began to feel lost and scared.

I continued to work at being a legal secretary. I say *worked at* because it was a difficult profession in which to reach any heights unless you were thin and attractive, well dressed, single and socially adept. I was none of those things, except for being single, per se. I'm not sure I even knew the proper fork with which to eat a salad. I was from a small town, and I wasn't sophisticated enough to know there were different forks for different foods. Between us, we had earned just enough to survive, and sometimes barely, and now there was just me. I had to budget every penny and there weren't enough of them to go around. I shopped at bargain stores, purchasing Jersey chemise dresses that came in different colors and I would alternate them throughout the week. The backless white heeled pumps would also be worn down to a nub by the time I had been working at this firm for three months, but I continued to wipe them clean every morning before work, dabbing over the scuffs with white shoe polish. On my meager budget, I couldn't even afford a new pair of shoes.

I liked my job, even though there existed somewhat of a competition with the other secretaries who were far more experienced in Arizona law than I was. The firm worked on various types of cases, the most interesting being the Winnie Ruth Judd case, where Marvin Belli, hotshot legal mind of the era, was lead counsel. This granny-looking woman was dubbed the Trunk Murderess because she had been convicted of cutting up her lover, placing him in a footlocker and leaving it on the pier in San Francisco. At the time of the appeal it appeared that her mental state had deteriorated, and it was unlikely she would ever be granted a parole.

In the early fall of that year, with my own mental state deteriorating, out of the blue I finally began receiving letters and an occasional phone call from the absentee knight. He didn't ask too many questions and I didn't answer them. He sent me photographs of himself with handwritten notes on the back professing his love, and I used a Polaroid camera to shoot pictures of myself from the shoulders up to send him. (I was taking "selfies" long before they came into vogue around 2013.)

It wasn't until the end of November that we had a few short conversations about maybe getting married. Again, I'm assuming this decision was a difficult one for him and he could have very well walked away. But I'm thinking he must have been pressured by his parents to do the *right thing* (much like my own father had been.) Bombarded with an overabundance of beliefs that being an unwed mother was stigma enough, there was no way I was returning to Santa Fe in either condition, unwed or with child.

This particular self-imposed stigma of being pregnant and unwed was a direct parallel to the divorced person's automatic excommunication from the Catholic Church. You do not receive an official letter or a phone call from 1-800-THEVATICAN, but you *know* you've been ejected from the good graces of the church because you heard it broadcast from the pulpit often enough at Sunday mass. Although I'm certain my parents would have exchanged *I told you so* glances, they would have graciously accepted my plight. But frightened as I was, I lacked the courage to throw in the towel and return home. Besides, I'm not sure if I had yet come clean about exactly what I was doing in Phoenix and where was this teacher I had been traveling with.

My immediate boss at the firm was one of the senior partners and one morning he called me into his office, holding a sheet of paper in his hand. He explained that my wages had been garnished and added that he was concerned not only with my obvious predicament, but my preoccupation and an apparent lack of interest in my job. He also mentioned that because I had neglected to enter an important trial date on his calendar, they missed the pretrial hearing, and it had taken a great deal of effort to convince the judge and the opposing counsel to reschedule the date. The judge could have ruled in favor of the other party and our client would have had to pay huge damages. Fortunately, they were able to convince both of my obvious lack of legal skills, or so I assumed that was the basis of their defense, the incompetence of one of the junior secretaries.

Since he was pulling out all the stops, he added that my filing basket was overflowing and there might be other equally important documents in the pile, so he had the senior secretary go through it to make sure. Overwhelmed, I burst into tears and blurted out that the garnishment was the result of my car being repossessed and that I had been sued for the balance owed, and guess what, I was also pregnant. After his initial shock at the barrage of tears and the accompanying confession, through his kindness we were able to resolve the garnishment and lawsuit issues. In addition, he contacted his private investigator, Jim Parker, to get to work on arranging a marriage ceremony for B and myself.

I was grateful for his help but mortified that my work had come under severe scrutiny, not only by my boss, but by the other secretaries. Even though I could create legal documents without supervision, because of this lapse I began to question whether I could set things right, knowing that everything I did from that point on would be checked. None of the secretaries said anything directly to me, but I'm sure I was the subject of plenty of breakroom gossip, and my filing basket was regularly dissected.

A few days before Christmas, B arrived from Florida. With details arranged by my boss, we were married in a private ceremony at a prominent judge's residence on Christmas Day of 1965 when I was seven months pregnant. The bride wore black. There were no maids of honor, no best man, no pews lined with aromatic flowers and no classical music in the air as we walked down the non-existent aisle. I wasn't sure what I felt but was relieved that the word *unwed* had been removed from the imaginary label on my t-shirt.

When all the I-dos were said and done, there was no official celebration, no champagne toast or three-tiered wedding cake or shower of rice as we made our exit. We might have stopped for food at Jack-in-the-Box on the way to my small apartment on the outskirts of Scottsdale. No hearts and flowers here, not even sex for old time's sake. He departed the next day. By then he had been stationed at Homestead Air Force Base in Florida for several months. I had assumed he was still at basic training at some base in Texas.

It took an inordinate amount of time for him to get around to sending me the forms necessary to register for military benefits and base privileges. When I finally went to apply, the clerk at the base in Glendale looked up at me through her bifocals when she noticed my physical description on the form was incorrect. I was not 5'7" and blue eyed (which I recalled was the description of the girl in the hospital parking lot.) The woman corrected the blanks to 5'2" and hazel eyes and might have wondered what kind of husband couldn't even describe his wife accurately. I realized how little he knew about me. I might have just been a figment of his imagination as he might have been of mine.

14 | TOGETHER ALONE

I HAD BEEN ALONE FOR THE ENTIRE PREGNANCY, with my only human interaction being at work or quick excursions to the grocery store. During the week I wore those same three Jersey dresses, along with one affordable maternity dress that fit like a small camping tent. I showed up for work right up to the day before I went into labor and returned two weeks later. To say that childbirth was a horrific experience would be an understatement. I was completely naïve, and the obstetrician I had seen for several months provided little information of what to expect.

It was impossible to calculate my due date because I didn't know when I became pregnant. During each of those visits the OB would just say, *any time now.* For three more months of every waking moment I lived in fear, expecting to deliver without warning. As far as I knew I would walk into the hospital, pop the baby out and be on my way. I was completely unprepared for the many hours of painful labor, the constant probing of my female anatomy by everyone who came into the room, and the absolute isolation I experienced. Adding to my misery, the doctor who happened to be on call that night was a complete stranger, with a very uncaring bedside manner.

Embedded in my mind were the long periods of pain, delirium, and ear-piercing screams which seemed to be coming from someone else. I implored anyone who came into my room to allow me to go home. I wasn't ready for this. An onslaught of all my fears came barreling down the pike. Right then I wished I was back home in Santa Fe, inside the protective bubble I had chosen to leave the previous year.

Under the circumstances, I thought a large dose of drugs would have certainly been appreciated, although a saddle block was administered a few minutes before the birth of a baby girl. The staff at St. Joseph's Hospital on Thomas Road in Phoenix might still remember me, or surely there is a plaque on the wall to commemorate the event, since I'm sure my discomfort shook the walls. Three days later a coworker picked us up at the hospital and I was grateful that my mother and sister would soon be coming from Santa Fe to spend a few days.

Some months before, I had occasion to meet my in-laws when they visited two of their daughters enrolled at Arizona State University in Tempe. They stopped by to meet their newest granddaughter shortly after her birth. Three months later my husband in absentia would meet her in person. The same Air Force which I naively believed didn't allow correspondence during basic training apparently also didn't allow prospective fathers a furlough for childbirth. Whether he had even inquired about the possibilities remained a mystery, and I pretended not to care, but I did. Had he been around to hold my hand and offer comfort, the entire birth experience might not have been so traumatizing. As part of the fairy tale, I believed childbirth should be a wonderful bonding event between two people in love. I've often wondered if his absence was cultural rather than personal. I didn't have an answer for that either.

Somewhere along the line I gave up being passively adrift and became actively engaged in staying afloat. I was as unprepared for parenthood as I was for marriage. I felt scared and abandoned, and I was angry that I had allowed someone to treat me as though I meant nothing. On the other hand, I was far more apprehensive of being alone with a newborn, and it didn't take very long to shove all my indignation back into the appropriate compartment in my head.

I was surprised to learn B had requested a furlough to return to Phoenix and take us back to live in Florida. By the end of two weeks, we had purchased a used car, packed everything up, and headed to Miami to live out the rest of his enlistment. Traveling with a three-month old was daunting, to say the least. She bawled most of the way. We drove almost non-stop through so many states that it became a blur and arrived in Florida in record time. We found an upstairs apartment in South Miami and within a week I was employed at a Coral Gables law firm.

At the firm, each of the three attorneys specialized in a different field. My salary was higher than that in Phoenix, but it required creativity in stretching out a certain amount of money to cover a higher cost of living and expenses which also included childcare. A soldier's pay didn't amount to much, but there were benefits at the commissary where food prices were less, and medical care was free. It could be said we lived an almost meaningless existence, and I say that in the most meaningful way possible. Once again, we had not formulated a plan. We were just there, waiting to finish being there, so we could be somewhere else. Another shockwave ran through me when I discovered I was again expecting a child which resulted in a similar birth experience because he had to work that night, and that October I gave birth to another daughter, alone in a military hospital again surrounded by strangers.

My life was formulaic: get up, get dressed, feed the kids, go to work, pick up the kids, come home, feed the kids, and go to bed. For the life of me I wonder why B hadn't thought to just drop us off in Santa Fe where at least there would have been family support. I guess the subject never came up. We were in a section of the country so different from New Mexico it boggled my mind. You could drive from one end of Santa Fe to the other in fifteen minutes. In Miami, fifteen minutes would get you three blocks if you managed to hit every traffic light.

Three years, four hurricanes and a second daughter later, B was honorably discharged. That week he collected his early discharge bonus and as I set the dinner table a few nights later, he casually dropped a bomb in my midst. He'd decided he wanted to remain in Florida, but without us. I felt sideswiped. There had been no discussion or acknowledgement of his discontent in the marriage. I had focused on getting through the expanse of months before we would return either to New Mexico or Arizona, where at last we would continue our life as a family. I was not prepared for this turn of events, which he related without emotion.

Other than driving to work and to the sitter across town, I was not an experienced city driver. I couldn't even imagine driving on my own with two small children across what was foreign countryside to me. The distance to Santa Fe was two thousand miles, and I would have to drive through seven states. I feared getting lost and knew it would take more than a week, barring any mechanical problems or a complete nervous breakdown. By air, the cost for one adult and two children was prohibitive, and I quickly crossed that off as an option. I had only traveled by air once in my life, a white-knuckle flight from Phoenix to Albuquerque in a heavy rainstorm, and I wasn't looking forward to repeating that traumatic event again. Now I'm certain I was suffering from fully developed phobias about flying and driving, let alone wide-open spaces in a car with two toddlers. With all the stress and anxiety brought about by these events, I certainly could have used a padded cell to scream into.

I packed the children's clothes and a few necessities and boxed up what we would leave behind. I assumed he would keep the apartment, but I gave it a good cleaning anyway. Without further explanation, at the last-minute B decided he would take us back to Arizona, and once there we would figure out the next move (or so I assumed.) We traded in our roach-infested car (really) for a similar make and didn't have to take the pesky bugs home with us as passengers. Several years of fast food and cookie crumbs had resulted in an infestation under the seats and in the trunk, but a thorough vacuuming before trade-in pretty much erased all evidence, for at least long enough to close the deal.

I breathed a sigh of relief as we left Florida, a place which had provided little nourishment to my soul. I didn't share his obvious soft spot for fishing off the bridges on a hundred-mile stretch to Key West, where we observed giant Grouper swimming along as if in slow motion; or the sight of thousands of disenfranchised blue crabs crossing the highway to Homestead Air Force Base after a hurricane. There was little comfort provided by the fear and devastation thrust on a Santa Fe girl by hurricanes named Beulah and Gladys, both of which threatened to blow the roofs off houses and send one-ton automobiles flying into swimming pools.

No, I did not have a tender space in my heart to store the memories of the preceding three years. The compartments to which I relegated my thoughts and emotions were already overflowing, and there was no room at the inn.

15 | ON THE ROAD AGAIN

On our return journey west, we would cross those seven states repeating in reverse the same route we had traveled three years before. Giant Cypress trees reaching into the darkness across Louisiana byways made for eerie night travel, their roots clinging to the edge of the narrow roadway, in my imagination beckoning images of multi-armed creatures. At long last we pulled into my parents' driveway in Santa Fe. I was eager for them to meet their two granddaughters and son-in-law, even though I could not guarantee he would be in our lives much longer. I didn't care. I was *home.* I had missed the small-town comfort as opposed to the go-go-go atmosphere of Miami and Phoenix.

It was immediately apparent to me that my parents were not suffering in the slightest from any form of empty-nest syndrome. They seemed to flourish in the fact that all my siblings had essentially flown the coop and had lives of their own. When my father retired from his job in Los Alamos, they were able to devote their time fully to their small cottage industry. At their kitchen table they created handcrafted tin items for local museum and gift shops. They were becoming well known in the traditional art field for reviving patterns and designs from 19th century New Mexico on tin plate. The tender embraces my mother gave me brought me to tears. It had been such a long time since I felt loved.

I thrived on being around family. The weather in Santa Fe was cool, and my childhood home on West Houghton Street was welcoming and peaceful. The giant apricot trees in the front and back yards were about to bloom, as was the perpetually wormy apple tree. The aromas that I had yearned for while in Arizona and Florida came wafting from the kitchen stove through the house. I was intrigued how easily my mother bonded with the girls, having seen the older one for only a few days after her birth. With little effort, she shifted from artist to mother and prepared dinner for additional guests. Our first meal there might have been ordinary, but to me it was special: pinto beans simmered on the gas stove all day, served with red chile and flour tortillas. There had been no substitute in other states, nothing even close. At a Cuban restaurant in South Miami, the enchilada plate on the menu was so far from that in New Mexico it wasn't even palatable. It was a true homecoming, and I prematurely dreaded the thought that in a few days we would be leaving. The girls spent their waking hours outside in the yard, sitting in the shade of the apricot tree, holding on tight to my mother's two adopted Siamese cats.

B also appeared to enjoy being there, having received a genuine welcome from my parents and siblings, and perhaps feeling there might be a valid reason in his mind to hold our small family together for just a while longer. I was still wearing my rose-colored glasses, as he too seemed content and at peace as he visited a local art store to stock up on supplies. In a world of his own, he spent his idle time painting a group of canvases, one of which still resides in a corner of my basement, and a small still life of purple onions that sits on my kitchen counter. There was no denying that my parents' creative energy in the daily production of their handcrafted tinwork had renewed the artistic fervor which had laid dormant since his years at IAIA.

My parents began each day with a simple breakfast. Mother prepared oatmeal and buttered toast while my father spooned precise tablespoons of coffee into the stovetop percolator. I smiled, listening to him as he hummed an old New Mexican ballad as he adjusted the heat on the burner. Their workday began following breakfast. With heavy metal shears, he snipped away at patterns for tin mirror frames, light-switch plates and Kleenex box holders, all of which they would spend the day tapping intricate designs on the surface. He would solder joints as necessary, and once the items were completed, they would be packed in boxes and delivered to the individual or gift shop that ordered them. Their only break was for lunch, after which he napped. That afternoon, as my mother prepared the dinner meal and set the table, my father relaxed with a couple of bottles of Budweiser and the afternoon newspaper. There appeared to be a calm in the air which I had not experienced during my childhood.

As our visit came to an end, without discussion we packed up the kids and prepared to depart. Without verbal agreement, it appeared we were going to try to make a go of it, and I was willing to take the chance. With tearful goodbyes, I hesitated for a microsecond and wondered if I should consider staying put. We arrived in Phoenix the next day and rented a small one-bedroom apartment near the airport. The noise was deafening, and I quickly understood why the rent was so reasonable. It was about this time that I began to experience episodes of floating anxiety. I was cooped up for days at a time with two exuberant toddlers, and without a vehicle. The constant roaring of jets flying overhead added to my misery. I can't say I received much in the way of emotional support from B, who had enrolled at ASU courtesy of a BIA grant from the tribe and spent more hours on campus than I believed necessary.

Months later when we received his severance pay from the military, we put a down payment on a house far from the airport. It was a nice house in a nice neighborhood, perfect to pursue the perfect marriage and the perfect family. As we settled in our new surroundings in Tempe, a fledgling community bordering Scottsdale, he continued classes and I took a job with a downtown law firm and found a babysitter in our neighborhood. Life was moving forward quicker than a snail's pace.

When things are quiet, I tend to assume that everything is progressing as it should be. My ability to slip in and out of denial provided the vehicle to keep me afloat. As that year came to an end, the grant checks from the BIA became smaller each month. Confused, I contacted the tribal office to complain about their obvious error. It turned out he had stopped attending classes some months before and assistance was adjusted downward. I felt like a disciplinarian when I approached the subject. One thing was certain, he needed to find a job and start helping out. We were drowning in living expenses and I couldn't find a way to alleviate that burden. That weekend, I shifted into fixit mode and spent an entire day on the phone contacting every airline company in the Yellow Pages to inquire about employment. Because of his military experience in fueling jets, I secured an interview for him with Air West, a small airline later purchased by billionaire Howard Hughes, where he would be employed for several decades.

16 | RESERVATIONS REQUIRED

Since B was of Hopi Indian ancestry, I had always imagined life on an Indian reservation would be much different than city life and that he might have had to adjust when he was transferred from freshman year at NAU in Flagstaff and enrolled at the school in Santa Fe. Even after our years together, he had yet to take us to visit his family in Parker. Was it me or was it just because I perceived myself as an outsider? Like many Spanish families, I wondered if they, too, preferred their children marry inside their own culture. Our children had not yet spent any quality time with their Hopi/Miwok grandparents. Perhaps reading my thoughts, finally, one summer day we loaded up the truck and traveled the several hundred miles for a visit. Arriving there, I was surprised how different the landscape was from the city, and more so how different from pueblos and reservations in New Mexico.

The Colorado River Indian Reservation was developed in 1865 by combining five tribes surrounding the Poston/Parker area bordering the Colorado River. In the 1940s, members of the Hopi and Navajo tribes in southeastern Arizona were then relocated to the site. B was born in Flagstaff shortly before the relocation commenced. The reservation was just like any other small town or village in the southwest. Unlike pueblos in New

Mexico, there were no flat-roofed adobe houses with small mud ovens in the yard for daily or weekly bread baking. There were no vendors wearing turquoise necklaces and sterling silver beads around their necks, hawking their wares to tourists. And there were no rolled-up handwoven rugs used for sleeping on the floor or recently-fired pots for distribution to tourists and museum gift shops. Instead, the vast countryside was peppered with pitch-roofed houses with indoor plumbing, electricity, television sets and abundant acreage around them, fields heavily planted with alfalfa. My in-laws' residence on a dusty dirt road in Poston resembled any wood-framed tract home in Middle America. The furnishings were modest, but comfortable, and no different than what we had in our own home. The summer heat index was comparable to Phoenix, if not a bit higher, reaching as much as one hundred eighteen degrees on any given summer day.

The extended family gathered together for dinner almost every evening during the week, except for Friday when the men would all disappear to a watering hole in nearby Parker. Shortly before sunset, we would scour the fringes for mesquite wood and pile it near the shed while one of the men started a fire in a shallow pit covered with a large sheet of thick screening. When the coals began to glow, cuts of beef, mutton and chicken were set on the grill. My mother-in-law, a sweet Miwok/Mission Indian with an endearing smile, foil-wrapped fresh corn and russet potatoes and placed them on the coals. The meat was grilled until tender, and the corn and potatoes unwrapped and slathered with butter and salt. There was plenty of beer passed around as everyone sat on the ground or on benches to enjoy the feast. Roars of laughter accompanied trips down memory lane as stories flowed. Courtesy of one of the old Hopi aunties, the children later munched on *piki,* light, fluffy sheets of blue cornmeal, flash-cooked over a hot griddle. This was a melt-in-your-mouth cultural snack carried down through the generations and not available at your local grocery store.

Since the weather in Arizona tends to be murderously hot in the summer, we usually visited in the spring and fall. B and the girls spent long hours swimming in the culverts of the Colorado River and the adjacent canals. Having never learned to swim, I preferred to sit next to the evaporative cooler in the kitchen. One spring day we attended a rodeo in Parker, and it was not unlike the one held annually in Santa Fe, with the exception that this was an all-Indian rodeo. Either way, it wasn't the type of activity I enjoyed. It was much like watching baseball—too much time elapsed between innings, while I sat on the bleachers and roasted in the searing sun. When the rodeo was over, the crowd headed to an indoor barbecue/dance event, where the featured guest was Jay Silverheels (better known as the Lone Ranger's sidekick Tonto). I felt odd to be the only non-native person in the building and I wondered if my husband felt equally odd being with that person. Leaning against the wall, I felt out of place, while Silverheels basked in the adulation heaped on him by fans of all ages.

My husband was a different person around his family. They constantly joked around and he never missed an opportunity to use his sharp wit as a retort. I found it refreshing to listen and laugh at the stories they told and the fun they poked at each other. On the drive back to Phoenix, a thought crossed my mind. *Where did this persona retreat to when we were home, and why? Did he prefer reservation life to city life?* I would never know the answers to my questions because I never thought to ask.

17 | A FALL FROM GRACE

THE TEMPERATURE IN PHOENIX was over one hundred fifteen degrees in the underground parking lot as I exited the elevator three levels beneath the law offices where I worked. I unlocked the door to my car and slid into the driver's seat. Clutching the steering wheel, I started the engine, backed up and sped up the levels, suddenly barely able to breathe. I knew I was dying. My heart was racing, and I felt as though the five-story building above me was going to collapse on my head. I raced through the parking levels until I pulled out onto the busy street and headed home. My knuckles were white as I felt something awful taking over my mind and body. I couldn't think straight. At every intersection I prayed for the red light to turn green, only to hit another after a few blocks. I was fifteen miles from home, and I wasn't sure I could make it. Somehow, I found myself at my front door, turning the key as my children jumped with delight. I sat on the couch, trying to slow my thoughts down to a whisper, urging them to watch TV for a while so I could rest for a moment.

With my husband on night shift, I slept fitfully, reliving the fear and panic throughout the endless hours. The next day I reported for work and while my boss was in court, I called at least fifteen doctors and finally reached one who would see me that afternoon.

Within a few moments of observing the state I was in, he instructed me to go home and take eight of the ten milligram pills he prescribed. I walked out of the pharmacy clutching the prescription, my knees weak and my hands shaking. Another eternity passed and I was home. The plastic bottle contained fifty black and green capsules of a drug called Librium. I was hesitant to take the amount the doctor prescribed. I was more frightened of this than I was of dying. I took only one. The insert read that this particular drug was used to treat symptoms of fear and anxiety and withdrawal from alcoholism. I knew I had two of those symptoms.

There was nobody to whom I could turn for comfort—someone who understood what I was going through, since I didn't understand it myself. As I sat on the couch in the living room, my husband glanced at me in exasperation as I swallowed one of the capsules. I could no more explain to him what was happening because I didn't have the words. What I did know was that for the entire month preceding that moment, I had slept very little and spent most of my time in a state of exhaustion, anxiety and fear. It was apparent to me that his was a black and white world, a get-over-it-world where you willed yourself well. I wasn't sure if this was just *his* way or the way most Native Americans approached life. I thought his attitude was cold and heartless, one which seemed to render him brain dead when another's emotional issues drifted to the surface and begged for support. I hoped he had the compassion to assure me I would be okay, but that was a misconception on my part.

The effects of anxiety trickled into my workday. I realized the need to slow down and spend more time with myself and my children. I quit the downtown job where the women in the secretarial pool spent more time looking down their noses at me than they did at their desks. Thinking a change would be beneficial, I took a job with an attorney I had known from a previous firm, although his office was on the west side and twenty miles from home. The two-lawyer firm was a one-person stenographic situation. I was in charge of everything except for the bookkeeping and probably my life. The positive aspect of the change was short-lived. For the next few months, I existed solely on caffeine and very little else, which triggered more rapid heartbeats. Anxiety ruled my life and dictated my every move. I found excuses to stay home any time I could get away with it, citing a whole list of imaginary ailments.

This condition would cause me to abandon grocery carts full of a week's provisions in the middle aisle of the store when I couldn't take another step forward. The ceiling was falling in and the walls were compacting. I imagined I was going to fall dead at the checkout counter. I was so anxious while at work I couldn't close the door to the bathroom. One time I even asked our middle-aged Baptist-with-a-southern-drawl -holier than-thou bookkeeper if she would stand by the bathroom door while I was in there and she looked at me as if I had just landed from Mars. When she rolled her eyes, I felt ashamed and belittled. She didn't take the time to ask why or try to comprehend my state of mind and my sudden fear of enclosed places. Was that an attitude typical of Southern Baptists, or just hers?

My bosses were concerned about my health (and I imagine my sanity). After I experienced several piggy-backed attacks where my heart raced over 200 BPM while I attempted to explain away this transient fear which pierced my head on a daily basis, they scheduled an appointment with a client of theirs, a psychiatrist with offices nearby. My boss drove me there, fearing I couldn't even make the four-block trip on my own, and left instructions with the receptionist to call him when I was done. I sat on the couch in the waiting room, trying to maintain calm as I thumbed through an innocuous women's magazine offering yet another magic overnight product to lose ten pounds. I had easily dropped twenty pounds in the previous three months and was down to a size eight dress in a manner I wouldn't have recommended to anyone. Moments before I was called into the doctor's office, I was ready to give it all up and go running out the door. I would have, had I not been driven there by someone else.

I spent half an hour describing to this stranger the thoughts which filled my mind and the overwhelming fear and feelings of desperation. I feared going off the deep end with no-one I could count on to pull me back. He wanted to know what was going on in my life, in my marriage. Couldn't he see I had a brain tumor or some other horrible affliction? What did my marriage have to do with anything? Marriage was marriage, that's all. We were normal. I was normal. My children were normal. We even lived on a street called Normal Avenue. He slid the tissue box in my direction as I burst into tears. My life had spiraled to a dizzying place, and I had nowhere to turn.

In a nutshell, the psychiatrist gently explained that I was suffering from the effects of a great deal of stress, a condition for which I had never developed coping skills. He said that as a result of the accumulation, I was now unable to deal with even the slightest shift in my life and was in a panic about things both large and small, with or without reason. As he spoke, I felt my heart rate slowing down and my hands stop shaking. When the appointment came to an end, he scribbled out a prescription for Valium, along with a sample pack to tide me over. He handed me a glass of water and made me swallow one before I left his office.

The daily dose began to take effect as days passed and provided an entirely different outlook than that of past months. I slowly regained some normality in my life. I returned to my job, back to preparing stacks of legal documents required to keep the criminal elements which the firm represented out of jail. These clients paid cash up front for their defense and the small law firm began to move within a wider circle, becoming well-known for their courtroom successes in criminal law. I found the work enjoyable and exhilarating, each day presenting something different. One month it was my job to investigate if the ex-wife of a wailing country singer had secretly remarried in Nevada so he could cut off her alimony payments; the next month it was delivering papers to a client in the state prison at Florence, where once those steel doors clanked shut behind me, I had to close my eyes, take a deep breath and push myself forward.

I had the same problems with elevators, and even today when I have occasion to be on an escalator, I still feel as though I'm going to topple over backwards, causing me to grip the handrail even tighter. As my life began to mellow out, there were days when I felt a million miles from Santa Fe. A part of me still longed for the safety and comfort of home. Other times I didn't even think about it. I still called my parents every couple of weeks to make sure things were going well with them. They were in their mid-fifties and looking toward eventual retirement which would allow them to focus full time on their craft. Two tin sunburst mirrors created in their workshop hung my living room and served to remind me of home and the creativity and art which continued to flourish there. I still treasure them.

18 | NOT TONIGHT, DEAR

How does a person operate within the boundaries of a life that has obviously created so much tension and anxiety? The recent emotional crisis had been a turning point, and I had to repeat to myself that I was stronger than I believed I was. I'm not sure I was able to convince myself of anything at that stage. My children were growing up fast and were being deprived of a mother's nurturing, but I could barely nurture myself. Both enrolled in elementary school, they were spending the remainder of their day with a babysitter down the street, coming home for dinner and then off to bed. I spent weekends catching up with laundry and household chores, but the house always looked like a torpedo hit it.

B and I had not discussed or even admitted to any problems in our marriage, and he didn't pretend to understand my current emotional state. He was still enmeshed in the multiple shades of black which made up his perception of life. We allowed the status quo to remain until at whatever point we would be forced to talk about it. There were times when I felt peaceful enough, safe and confident enough to set the prescription aside. I had fewer anxiety attacks as time passed and eventually tossed the bottle in a drawer, where it would remain in place for over a year.

On a follow-up visit with my physician, he took me off birth control pills as they had been triggering both migraines and other issues. He cautioned me to not engage in intimacy until a more appropriate birth control method could be put into place as he surmised my body would be ultra-fertile. Although my husband was aware of this advice, he chose to ignore it and I conceived another child on Memorial Day. Our son was born on the exact day he was due, February 24 of the following year.

That Wednesday in February was particularly memorable. B scoffed when early that morning I mentioned I was going into labor. A keepsake from our life at the base, I had an old altimeter with a second hand which kept extremely accurate track, and I insisted that I had been in labor since the previous night. He guffawed as he said I was imagining things and went off to work at six that morning. My father-in-law happened to be in Phoenix for a tribal council meeting and he stopped by at eight-thirty with an hour to kill before his appointment. I fixed him a cup of coffee and told him I was in labor. He asked why B hadn't stayed home and I made the excuse that he had a meeting at work which he couldn't miss. He promised that if I couldn't reach his son by noon that day, he would take me to the hospital.

Grandpa Moody, as my children called him, came by exactly at noon and drove me to the new Phoenix Indian Hospital and then returned to his meeting. My son was born half an hour later at 12:35 PM and one of the nurses announced he was the thirteenth baby born in this new facility. The recovery room in the maternity ward was full, so while the space was cleared, an orderly pushed my bed into the hallway where I could see visitors and staff pass back and forth. As I laid on the bed against the wall, my heart began to pound out of my chest. Suddenly, I was afraid and didn't know why. I could hear the ticking of the clock on the wall as the minute hand circled around in slow motion. I tried to relax, fearing something had gone wrong because of the birth, and broke into a cold sweat. I felt so alone. The hospital staff paid no attention to me as they whizzed by. A nurse passed by my bed and I reached out to her and told her of my discomfort. She said the room was ready and called an orderly to take me there. I felt a sense of relief; not because of the room, but because I was not alone for those few minutes.

For the next two days, I tried without success to contact my husband, and when I finally reached him, it was time for me to be released. He gave no explanation for his absence. The nurse gave me a *poor thing* look as she wheeled me out into the sunshine, clutching the newborn in my arms. I realize now I had experienced yet another anxiety attack, brought about by the fact that I had just given birth to our third child, and it was the third time he had chosen not to be a part of it. He appeared emotionally detached from the birth, as though this was all my doing and he had no part in it. I knew very little about Native American culture, but I wondered again if this was part of the belief that a pregnant woman was expected to be left alone in a field to pop her baby out and then return to her chores without missing a beat. Little did I know he would spend the better part of our marriage distancing himself from not only me, but from our children as well.

19 | CLUES FOR THE CLUELESS

My assumption that my husband had been brought up in similar folds of family as I had was a delusion. I would learn much later that from a young age, along with hundreds of other Native American children, he was enrolled at a Presbyterian Mission boarding school in Ganado, Arizona. Sometimes as much as a year would pass without him ever going home to see his family, or them coming to see him. In more recent research, I would also learn that many of these students had been abused and molested, and others forced to do backbreaking labor without pay. In adulthood, he was hauling his own baggage and I had been willing to overlook it because I didn't know what the bags contained and I'm not sure I cared. He appeared to be an introvert and saw only the black and the white. His was not a Technicolor life. He was creative, intelligent, and in later years, well-read and still had an uncanny wit which could evoke laughter on one side and tears on the other. In the years we spent together, we danced the dance of magnets, only to find one repelled the other. The harder I held on, the harder he pushed me away.

Today, I believe I am equipped to better recognize the signs, but at that time I was so intent on keeping our family together I continued to be oblivious. We had become good friends with our babysitter and her husband, so when they moved thirty miles from our neighborhood, we attended a housewarming at their new home in Mesa, Arizona. Lots of alcohol and pot-smoking went on that night and I was derided for not participating. Not only was it not my thing, but my children and hers were in the house. I assumed I would be driving home, but that didn't happen. The girls were going to stay for a slumber party, so we said our goodbyes and piled into the truck, our toddler son between us. B insisted on driving, even though I protested to no avail. I began to pray as we headed toward the first exit to the Black Canyon Highway and suddenly found us tearing down the wrong side of the road doing 95 mph. He burst into laughter as he saw the fear on my face and drove even faster. I couldn't get him to slow down until there were several headlights coming straight at us. For an instant he came to his senses and turned the truck around so we could exit the highway. I held my breath for the remainder of the trip, which was still too fast for my comfort. I was grateful to be home, still holding on to my son for dear life.

I had often heard that things happen for a reason, including unpleasant surprises. I didn't need any more surprises in my life. I just wanted to be happy. Some months later my car was out of commission and in a rush to make it to work on time I decided to take his truck. Since he still worked the night shift, I knew he would sleep most of the day. I searched his trousers for the keys and then went out to the carport to check under the seat of the truck. Along with the keys surfaced a gold gift box containing a pair of silver earrings which he must have created at his workbench while I was at work. I didn't have pierced ears, so I knew they weren't for me. Stuffed behind the seat was a plastic bag containing a neatly-folded cowboy shirt, Levis and boots. Other clues which had hidden in plain sight confirmed that for the months stretching back to my last pregnancy, he had evidently been having an affair. I sat behind the wheel of the truck for the longest time feeling like a fool.

In most relationships there are final straws. Mine was no different. One night after keeping dinner warm for longer than I considered reasonable, I fed the children and put them to bed. I called the sitter to watch them while I went to pick up an imaginary prescription, then got in my car and drove down Seventh Street and pulled into the parking lot of a popular lounge, filled to the edges with a wide variety of pickup trucks. The patrons were mostly Native Americans, interspersed with women young and younger, all looking for a free drink, someone to dance with and maybe a one-nighter.

The band played with fervor, twanging out popular country songs and a few Creedence hits thrown in for good measure. As the music ended and the throng sidled over to their tables, I spotted him in the crowd and watched as he walked next to an attractive long-haired Native American woman and directed her to the chair next to his. For a moment I couldn't breathe, and tears burned the corners of my eyes. I had gone there to lay my suspicions to rest once and for all and the proof of the pudding sat before me. My first inclination was to justify what I had seen; that she was just a friend, or a friend of a friend; but when they stood up to dance a slow dance, I knew they hadn't just met. They both had a one-nighter look on their faces.

Although my tendency was to forgive or overlook a situation, I wasn't willing to stifle my emotions this time. He had proven himself to be a closet philanderer and too secretive to admit to other women that he was married and the father of three. It brought to mind a time years before when I had contacted the USAF base to speak to him and the Private who answered asked who was calling. When I identified myself as his wife, he bellowed with laughter and said *you gotta be joking; the Chief ain't married.* He thought I was some woman chasing a soldier, snickered and hung up.

I kept everything inside until that weekend and then dragged it all out in the open. He was neither remorseful nor apologetic. The obvious options weighed heavily on my mind. We could separate, divorce, or continue to live the lie. I felt myself plummeting into fear mode, afraid to face a decision which would severely affect not only myself but our children. I factored in the differences which clearly existed between us, but could find nothing to satisfy the question of *why?* Why would he do something that would place our marriage in jeopardy? Did he really believe I would turn the other cheek and forgive him? *Did he really not love me enough to work things out?* Breaking up didn't seem right. It didn't go with my fantasy storyline. But what's a soon-to-be-divorced mother of three to say, that we were victims of our upbringing? Neither of us had an idyllic childhood. I was beginning to wonder who did.

We divorced within the year, and once again the turmoil I avoided for so long resurfaced. I was thirty-one years old with three young children. Although we could have chosen to separate and live apart, the divorce proved to be more traumatizing than I had imagined. *How was I going to manage?* The relationship was irreparable, and I saw no need to continue the charade. Neither of us had the necessary tools or the skills to use them to save our marriage. We had stayed together for some unknown reason; security, familiarity, but probably not love. The adhesive that kept us glued together had dissolved. Once again, that elusive white knight rode off into the sunset without me, this time headed in the direction of another castle.

20 | ROMEO, ROMEO, WHEREFORE ART THOU?

After the divorce, I continued to work at another downtown Phoenix area two-lawyer firm specializing in criminal and family law in the same building I had left years before to move to Miami. Of the two attorneys, one was more flamboyant than the other, who although somewhat attractive was a bit overweight and as I recall, married. I don't know what kind of unintentional vibe I was giving off, but one day he invited me to lunch and said we could finish the bookkeeping later that afternoon. We ate at a small restaurant on Grand Avenue a few miles from the office. I was surprised to learn he had a great sense of humor as we covered many subjects during the meal, often breaking into gales of laughter.

After lunch, we headed back in the direction of the office, but instead he drove into the parking lot of the Ramada Inn on Seventh Street. I assumed he was stopping to pick up or deliver legal documents. When he opened the passenger side door, I said I would wait, and he said *I can't do this without you.* I thought maybe I needed to notarize a document, so I grabbed my purse and followed him into the lobby. That was a mistake. Apparently, he already had a room reservation and from the shocked look on my face and my apprehension in moving toward the elevator, he must have gotten the message. He turned and walked back to the car, slid into the driver's seat and drove back to the parking garage and pulled into his space with an abrupt slam of the brakes. He barely turned his head when he said he would be in later, although he must have entered through the side entrance, because I didn't see him until I was leaving work that evening.

After that, things between us were strained, but I don't recall an apology or an explanation. This appeared to be typical conduct for the times. All around me I observed long-married attorneys take long lunch hours with both receptionists and clients. Without batting an eyelash, they would repeat the process whenever the opportunity arose. Of course, I could have pretended to be interested in his overtures, but I was aware of the ramifications of office affairs. I had observed that once the initial glow of the secret romance wore off, things could get hairy, especially when another woman came into the picture. Besides, what if this would have been just a one-time romp; and double besides, he was married. I think the fact that his law partner was such a playboy might have rubbed off on him and he was testing the waters, and I was the closest fish in the pond.

I should have been on a basketball team. I was always good at rebounding. Breakups were earth shattering, but I never hesitated to jump right back into the fray. Unaccustomed as I was to being alone, after the divorce I renewed the subconscious search for the knight. My children kept me company, but they were what they were: three small individuals whom I had left to their own devices, mostly because I believed children raised themselves. I didn't know any better. At that time I wasn't in need of or expecting intellectual stimulation. I was looking for the somewhat elusive person who wanted me for who I was, and right then I was willing to settle for anything, anybody, because I had no idea who I was or what I was looking for. *Does that make sense?* To be at that age, twice divorced and not have a clue as to what you're looking for or what you need in your life? Surely by now I would have learned the purpose of some of the lessons I'd been handed. But I ignored those too. I had no interest in becoming someone's appendage, but I longed to belong—short and sweet.

My three children were all under six years old, each barely self-sufficient enough to manage a breakfast of Fruit Loops or Coco-puffs and milk. On my meager budget and the words *child support* being only a figment of the court's imagination, finding a reliable babysitter to at least have an opportunity to go out clubbing occasionally was difficult. Every so often it would happen, though. At a legal seminar held in our building that summer I was befriended by two women, also legal secretaries, and we met up later at a club in Scottsdale. Over the weeks we became each other's lifelines, filling gaps and voids originally occupied by the men in our lives. The sisterhood of Misery Loves Company had been established.

In the 1970s, downtown Phoenix offered a wide and varied choice of nightclubs with an abundance of smoke, plenty of beer, mixed drinks, and ear-piercing music. Being a good dancer wasn't a requisite because for the prevailing music trend, couples only had to stand an arm's length apart, execute a few in-place foot and arm movements and sway to the tempo of Led Zeppelin, Creedence Clearwater Revival, The Eagles, and Fleetwood Mac hits performed by popular local bands. Renditions of *Proud Mary* and other John Fogarty hits generally brought the house down. Relationships with men we encountered lasted anywhere from a night to a month, rarely longer, but were a welcome diversion from the workaday world.

On one hot summer night, the three of us walked into a place on Scottsdale Avenue we assumed was a nightclub but turned out to be a piano bar, something I was unfamiliar with. The interior was dimly lit, and we debated about finding a table. Undaunted, we found a spot, ordered drinks, and spent time mulling over work gossip and our difficulty in meeting decent men. Peggy, the youngest of our group, was a tall semi-buxom blonde with cornsilk hair reaching down her back. Particularly fond of band members, without a second thought, she generally managed to glom onto one before the evening was up. In this instance, she set her sights on the piano player, who quickly succumbed to her wiles as she sat next to him on the bench and cuddled closer as he sang.

I don't think I was ever on the lookout for someone to take home for the night. I was just looking for adult conversation, nothing to do with Scooby-Doo, Holly Hobby or the Pink Panther. That's when I met J. He was a Robert Redford clone with deep blue eyes and sandy brown hair. He and his husky lumberjack friend sat down with us, and I thought for sure Mary would make a beeline across the table for him, but she didn't. She was telepathing a dreamy gaze across the room at a drop-dead gorgeous guy wearing a muscle shirt, who moments later joined us for just long enough to sweep her off her feet and transport her to a small table in a dark corner of the bar. And Peggy, who quickly tired of the piano player and never said no to a free drink, sat next to the lumberjack and left mister movie star for me. It might have been better to have considered him *Mr. Maybe* instead of *Mr. Right,* so as I smiled at this nice-looking man, I envisioned he might have the potential to ride a white horse.

It was obvious that our club members were searching for that indefinable relationship. Over time each of us would return to our comfort level: Mary cleared her bedroom drawers of all the sexy lingerie she had bought and returned to her ex-husband, a man who had not a clue as to why she left in the first place. Peggy would continue to date an attorney who set her up in a penthouse in downtown Phoenix and spent time with her as often as his wife allowed. At her young age, she had apparently already tired of the hunt and was willing to settle into a form of paid domesticity which suited her particular needs. As for me, I ventured into the uncertainty of a relationship with this new stranger.

As a couple, my new beau and I returned often to that piano bar and others, where he always sat close to the music and would break out in a song at the slightest prompting from the piano player. He knew all the words and melodies to hundreds of popular songs from the thirties to the fifties and sang them as though he had been singing them all his life. He was thirty-nine, but I suspected he was an old soul, and in another life should have been in Vaudeville. Night after night I sat and listened to music which was vaguely familiar, but never quite what I wanted to hear. Of course I was going to overlook that fact and do a commendable job of pretending I was loving every minute of it. J didn't reveal much about his relationships but one night mentioned in passing that for several years he had been living with an older woman. He gave no indication whether the relationship was romantic or platonic, or even current. One thing was certain, I wasn't desperate enough to date a man who was involved with another woman. I stopped answering his phone calls. He showed up on my doorstep one day, suitcases in hand and car parked in my driveway, and before too long transitioned quite easily into our lives.

My children were still young, but I caught a glimpse of raised eyebrows as they glanced at each other, communicating a silent code only they understood. I hadn't prepared them for the situation, but as per my normal course assumed they would take it all in stride. I never gave them credit for having the intelligence to require an explanation as to why this stranger was moving into their house and sleeping in their mother's bedroom. By that time, they had other confusion to deal with. Their father had married the woman he had an affair with and would soon be picking them up for a trip to the reservation to visit their grandparents, after which they would spend a month with him and his new wife in their new home on the other side of Camelback Mountain. I wondered how she felt being the new white person in the room.

21 | NORTHWARD BOUND

Late that spring, I phoned my sister in Idaho to catch up on events in our respective lives. I told her about J and she said we should come up for a visit. We hadn't seen each other for years and she was longing to spend time with family. The kids were with their father and J's tax work was seasonal, so he was off until February of the following year. I was in the process of selling the house in Phoenix and didn't have much equity coming from the sale, so once the deal was closed, I quit my job and we gathered up our belongings and headed for Idaho. I don't remember selling or giving away the furniture, and I know we didn't store it. We left his car parked out on the street and intended to pick it up once we decided where we were going to settle. Once again, I was playing all this by ear. I was part of a unit and willing to travel to the ends of the earth as long as the word *together* was part of the mix. Since leaving Santa Fe, I had traveled through more states than in my entire life before, but I was never traveling by myself—I was *with* someone.

Before I met J, I must have planned to return to NM with the few worldly possessions I could stash in the trunk, but that plan was apparently put on the back burner. In the blink of an eye, we settled into domesticity in Orofino, Idaho, a small town with a population of less than 500 inhabitants. It had the usual small-town elements: narrow streets, old historic buildings which included a courthouse and library, and quaint little houses. In the mid-1800s, Orofino was a gold mining camp near the Clearwater River and the Nez Perce Indian Reservation. It appeared not to have evolved much, with old buildings on Main Street still in use.

J loved the great outdoors and dreamed of someday settling down in Montana. Idaho was close enough. He could pretend he was a cowboy and if he needed to feel more authentic, a reservation was within driving distance. For a small town, Orofino had its scandals and gossip, and everyone knew who was doing what and who was doing whom. We were no exception, as we were the new couple in town and my sister and her husband were two of the better-known residents, so the curiosity meter peaked. My sister made sure we attended all the neighborhood barbecues and fishing events, and often invited us over for meals or just to hang out. They were as happy to have us in their midst as we were to be there. As much as I would have preferred beef, our first meal with them was roast bear, and would be repeated often in the many ways this particular animal could be prepared—meatballs, steaks, chops, burgers and the like. She had adapted well to what I considered a Little House on the Prairie lifestyle. I teased her that she probably swept her house with a corn husk broom purchased from a vendor in a horse-pulled wagon.

Since over time I had become a spur-of-the moment kind of person, we thought seriously about settling in Idaho and proceeded to rent a small house fairly close to my sister's. A huge fireplace built from river rock took up an entire wall in the living room and gave the house a log cabiny feel. There were plenty of trees and shrubs in the yard and lots of grassy space for my children to play and I was overjoyed knowing they would arrive from Arizona within a few weeks.

I took a job in the Orofino County Sheriff's Department with an honorary title of deputy, unlike that of my brother-in-law and sister who had worked in law enforcement for most of their thirty-five-year marriage. As bona-fide deputy sheriffs, they dressed in grey uniforms edged with black detail and packed fully loaded pistols. The local sheriff was a handsome, well-built man close to six and a half feet tall, and there was no disguising the fact that he occasionally plied sexual favors from women in custody who hoped to avoid jail time. That juicy item was part of the jailhouse speculation when he was out of earshot.

That Monday in July started off like every other Idaho day—crisp early morning summer breezes followed by an abundant dose of sunshine and warmth. Like most mornings, J left for his job at the local hardware store, the kids were with the sitter across town, and I arrived at the courthouse and prepared a quick breakfast for the inmates. Jail occupants weren't referred to as prisoners, because much like in the town of Mayberry and the Andy Griffith Show, most of them were local residents who had a little too much to drink or had accidentally on purpose shot a deer out of season, or some other minor infraction. Most were thirty-dayers waiting for their sentence to run out so they could dash over to the nearest water hole for a tall glass of beer. Cells in the jail room were small, surrounded by metal bars through which they could observe what was going on around them, another Mayberry setting. For the most part, they were friendly, and teased me relentlessly about the food I served.

Around noontime, I whipped up a batch of tuna salad sandwiches and arranged them on paper plates with a handful of potato chips and dill pickles on the side. The deputy on duty distributed the food as I clocked out and headed to the parking lot. I drove home, parked in the shade of the willow tree and entered the house. I kicked off my shoes and walked into the bedroom, intending to stretch out for a few minutes before fixing a quick lunch and returning to work.

As I sat on the edge of the bed and fiddled with the TV remote, I noticed the door to the closet in the corner was ajar. As the crime rate was virtually nonexistent, doors to houses were always left unlocked, so my first thought was that one of us had left it open rather than that someone had been in the house. Since it blocked the full view of the television set, I reached over to close it, only to discover all the clothes on J's side were gone.

22 | BEWITCHED, BOTHERED, AND BEWILDERED

TAKEN ABACK BY MY DISCOVERY, I was shocked and confused by this unexpected turn of events. What evil spell had been cast to throw me into this predicament; was there something in the air; something in the water? (Maybe I was cursed and needed to see a palm reader or a psychic but knew that was stuff frowned upon by my culture and the church, to which my brain was remotely attached.) Bitter tears stung my eyes as I blindly made my way through the tall grass and bushes down the path to my sister's house. I fell into her arms bawling my head off and was barely able to get the words out that he was gone, as in *not there anymore*.

While my sister brewed tea, my brother-in-law contacted the hardware store and learned that J had quit his job the previous Friday and stopped by early that morning to pick up his final paycheck. The three of us headed back to work, but I could barely function. I don't know which was worse, the devastated feeling or the thought of once again being alone. At mid-afternoon my sister mentioned that one of the patrol officers reported seeing J hitchhiking on the highway leading out of town that morning but thought nothing of it. He had on the treasured black cowboy hat he believed made him the cowboy he had always longed to be.

I picked my children up from the sitter's house and put on a happy face, telling them he had taken a trip to visit his family and would be gone for a while. I glanced with sadness at my three-year old son, who the week before had been the victim of J's idea of a haircut. This darling boy sported a Three Stooges look that appeared as if a bowl had been placed on his head and the hair trimmed off around it. My only consolation was that his beautiful locks would soon grow back. My bewildered state continued for days. From the time my kids arrived in Idaho, they behaved as though they were in a foreign country. They missed the hot Arizona climate and their friends in Phoenix. I began to wonder what was wrong with me. I had uprooted them, sold their house, and dragged them a thousand miles north to live with this person whom they probably still considered a stranger. We were in Idaho because my sister lived there and when we came to visit, we decided to stay and start a new life.

A few weeks before, we had picked them up at Lewiston Airport. They had barely adjusted to this strange land and being bounced around like basketballs. As I counted down the days when we would pick them up at the airport, J seemed more distant. Maybe he expected I would be willing to give up my children just to be with him. I wasn't. He never indicated that was an issue when they came to join us. I just assumed he would be as happy to see them as I was. In less than a month he was gone and I'm sure they wondered if they were the reason, but I assured them everything would be fine in the morning. Meanwhile, I continued to cry myself to sleep in the quiet of the night, hardly believing anything would ever be fine.

As attuned as I thought I was, I might have noticed a change in his demeanor the previous weekend when we were on a fishing trip on the Clearwater River after my brother-in-law sprung the idea that the Steelhead were biting. An hour or so into the picnic, I heard my middle daughter scream when a small avalanche of rocks rolled down the hill and trapped her hand beneath it. She was bleeding and in pain. I inspected her fingers for fractures and rinsed her hand with the icy river water. J barely looked up from his fishing pole and commented it was just a little cut and she would be fine. I insisted we should go to the ER, and he said he wasn't ready and repeated that it was nothing to be concerned about. Although putting on her bravest face, I could see my poor child was writhing in pain. With a sneer of disgust, he finally relented, noisily tossed his gear in the trunk and we took off. At the clinic, it took fourteen stitches to close the wound. He never apologized for his behavior or offered comfort in any manner.

A week after he left, I was on the phone pouring my heart out to my ex's new wife, the one he had the affair with; the one who I believed had so blatantly disrupted our lives. The bitch who had probably introduced him to theretofore not experienced sexual intimacies and then peeled him off the ceiling. (Yes, I was angry, but I kept it bottled inside. Heaven forbid anyone would see that side of me.) She flew into our small airport a few days later, spent the night and the next day boarded a plane with my children in tow while I watched from the sidelines. Was I doing what I had vowed to never do--giving my children up just to be with a man? I hoped not.

I hadn't yet formulated a plan and at that moment I didn't think I needed one. What I should have done was just taken my kids back to Santa Fe and left the rest to fate. But I didn't. My years of working in the legal field and with private detectives had provided me with a number of tools. I don't know what the hurry was. Letting him go and getting on with my life would have been the most reasonable plan, but there was nothing reasonable about it. I had made him my life. My brain has always stored insignificant facts and numbers I might not ever use, and as I sat at the kitchen table eating a bowl of misery soup, I recalled that J had often mentioned a bar in LA he liked to frequent. I reached for the phone and dialed information and a few minutes later I had the number I was looking for. On my next call, I found myself giving the bartender who answered the phone a quick description. "Oh, you mean the *cowboy?* Sure, hold on for a second." I held my breath as he came to the phone, surprised that I had found him. We had a short conversation, which didn't include the words *what are you doing and why did you leave me?* He said he was in the middle of a dart game and gave me a number where I could call him later. I should have wondered if darts was the only game he was playing, as I felt like the lowly pawn on a chessboard.

It may appear as if locating him in the huge metropolis of Los Angeles was a simple task, considering the million plus residents. It wasn't. I was relentless, determined, probably desperate, and frightened. I hunted him down like a five-star detective and I still didn't know what I was going to do when I found him. Why did I find it necessary to find him? Was it because I needed to convince him he had made a mistake by leaving? Or was it because I needed to know if he just might not have loved me.

Ready to jump back into the fray, within a few days I had packed up my belongings and was headed west on a road trip with my nineteen-year-old niece riding shotgun. Our quickly-conceived plan was for her to fly back from LA once I was settled there. When I called to let J know we had arrived, he said he already had plans for the evening. My niece and I stayed at a fleabag motel and the next afternoon drove to the house he shared with a friend. I couldn't tell if he was glad to see me or not and was feeling as though I had made another error in judgment. Again, I didn't have a Plan B, and Plan A was starting to look a little shaky. I breathed a sigh of relief when he agreed I could stay with him, and the next day we drove my niece to the airport. On the way there, we stopped at a strip mall where we bought her a slinky outfit and a pair of platform shoes, both high fashion for the seventies. After all, I thought that this might likely be the only time that small-town girl was going to be in the big city, having settled in the tiny town of Orofino when her parents relocated there.

23 | NIGHTLIFE IN THE CITY OF ANGELS

To my dismay, Los Angeles wasn't all that exciting, at least not from my perspective. It didn't take long to tire of sitting on a barstool and watch J playing darts until the place closed. We would arrive early in the afternoon, have a few beers and wait for everyone he knew to show up to compete in nightly dart competitions. Watching these small plastic missiles being hurled at a circular target on the other side of the room was as boring as watching ice melt. It was all I could do to keep from screaming and I soon discovered being together wasn't all that special. I felt like a concert pianist at a banjo convention.

After a few weeks of feeling like a third wheel in my own life and little or no affection or intimacy between us, I began to feel the strain of both the city and the meager attention. I realized I should have left well enough alone and stayed in Idaho until I could return to Santa Fe. I decided to gather up my remaining backbone and set out for home, although in the back of my mind I wondered how I could ever manage to drive all that distance by myself. I was terrified at the prospect. I still had never driven more than sixty miles alone. I didn't even know what highway led out of LA to get me to New Mexico, how far it was, and worse, what if the car broke down and I was left stranded. What was I going to do then? Apparently I was not as independent as I thought I was. As I loaded up my car, closed the trunk and watched him turn and walk back into the house, I found myself déjàvu-ing back to the same predicament in leaving Florida some years before.

I held back tears as I drove away, wound my way through several rundown neighborhoods while recalling someone in the bar had cautioned to be careful never to stray into the Compton area. I didn't know where that was, but it was frightening nonetheless. An hour later I pulled into a gas station and called J from a pay phone to tell him I was lost. That wasn't an exaggeration. I was emotionally lost. He directed me back to his place and I sat parked out in the street, not knowing what to do next. Perhaps I hoped he would draw a map so I could get home safely or follow me out to the highway, wherever that was. I looked up as he walked toward me, his suitcase in hand, and said he would drive me home. I was overwhelmed with emotion remembering the relief mixed with apprehension I felt in Florida. At the time, I didn't make the connection that both he and my ex-husband had a mean, sadistic streak to put me through almost identical incidents of potential abandonment followed by a quick reversal. A psychiatrist would have a field day dissecting this.

He slid into the driver's side, shifted into gear and minutes later we were at the city limits. Once on the road, J decided we might as well take a detour through Las Vegas. After a day of feeding nickels to the one-armed bandits and playing Blackjack, we drove out on the strip and while I marveled at the busy streets lined with thousands of bright lights, he drove into one of those white picket-fenced roadside wedding chapels you see in the movies. *Had he asked me to marry him?* No, but on the spur of that moment, he did suggest we might as well get married while we were there, since early on in our relationship I had mentioned my parents were old-fashioned and didn't believe in couples living together in sin. The fairy tale girl in me rationalized that perhaps this union was going to work out after all. We had an impromptu wedding ceremony in the small chapel. The sentimental person that he was, I'm sure on both our parts there were rings and tears of joy involved. I didn't care; I would have worn a cigar wrapper. This had certainly been an unexpected turn of events. I had no idea what had changed in his mind. Perhaps he also had the romantic notion that things might very well work out.

Later that week I was happy to once again be in Santa Fe. My parents were accepting of this blue-eyed Gringo I had pursued across several states before they met him. They were still enmeshed in their tinwork cottage industry, and their popularity as tinsmiths had grown by leaps and bounds since my last visit. My new husband expressed interest in their craft and tried his hand at cutting tin and tapping out designs with a metal punch and hammer. My parents seemed impressed by his creativity and willingness to learn. I too felt a glimmer of pride on seeing their reaction. Assuming we would be resettling in Santa Fe, I rented a suite of offices on Marcy Street in the downtown area with the small check from the sale of the Phoenix house and opened a secretarial service with my sister-in-law. J was to provide accounting services for clients and take care of our books. The business thrived over the remainder of the summer. Mid-October, the temperatures began to drop, the leaves were starting to turn, and the once-welcome breezes took on an icy chill. As I wrapped a borrowed sweater around my shoulders, I realized it had been years since I experienced a Santa Fe winter and didn't even own a warm coat.

One blustery autumn day my mother called the office and asked if I had seen J that afternoon. I assumed she needed something picked up from the store and told her I would take care of it. That wasn't it. Would it be a surprise to hear that it turned out to be another déjà vu moment? Earlier in the day when she went into the storage room where we kept our clothes, she noticed the door to the walk-in closet was ajar and that his side was empty. I couldn't believe my ears. I was reliving the moment when he left me in Idaho, the only difference was that I wasn't fifteen hundred miles from home. I was also dumbfounded that I had no clue this was going to happen.

Along with my parents, my brothers were also incensed that this Gringo had not only abandoned their sister but had taken my extra car as his getaway vehicle. At their urging I contacted the Arizona Border Patrol and provided a description of the vehicle and the license plate number. Late that evening an officer called to say J had been stopped at the border and was being detained until the stolen car report could be cleared up. Through several long conversations, he convinced them, and me, that as soon as our income tax check arrived next spring, he would send me the entire refund as payment for the car. Softhearted (and softheaded), I agreed, and he was allowed to continue his journey to Phoenix for the seasonal tax business coming up in a few months. I surmised he would again be out on the loose after April fifteenth.

For lack of a better term, I refer to this period of my life as an *interim marriage,* because it was over before it took roots. In my past I had a "not a marriage-marriage," an "almost marriage," and now an "interim marriage." We were married on an impulse. I hadn't been sure of how my parents were going to react when I came home with yet another man in tow, and now I wasn't sure how they were going to react to yet another breakup. In keeping with my forgiving nature, within a few months I returned to Phoenix to see him. This time I had a purpose—to serve him with divorce papers and from there drive into Scottsdale to retrieve my children. I hadn't seen them since they left Idaho. My deepest fear was that they might have forgotten me and thought I was never coming back. Overwhelmed with emotion, I vowed I would never be away from them again. It was a promise I was determined to keep.

When I saw him again that day in Phoenix, I realized nothing had changed in his life. He was still hitting all the piano bars and singing his heart out. He offered a half-assed explanation of why things hadn't worked out between us. *It wasn't about anything other than if we stayed together, there never would be any more firsts* . . . as if these firsts get used up, like heartbeats might but don't. In a quiet moment on the drive back to Santa Fe, I reflected with astonishment what he meant: first eye contact, first touch, first date, first kiss, first everything. I realized then that he lived in a fantasy world that had been far more complex than my own. Perhaps our divorce was also his first.

Empowerment seemed to slip in and out of my life without warning. This word was not a part of my vocabulary or a visible trait in my nature, but a feeling that I might just be strong enough to make it on my own. We would see. If things went downhill, at least I was home and had a lifeline to grab onto to keep from sinking.

24 | KISS A FROG, FREE A PRINCE

My children and I had returned to Santa Fe, my birthplace, the place I ran away from in my search for love. It would be cliché to say the city welcomed me with open arms—but I did feel the comfort of familiarity and family. There was no getting around the fact that I was a single parent with three children and the father, who apparently wasn't going to support them now that they were back in my fold. My parents' small adobe house was hardly big enough to accommodate four more family members, although somehow seven children and two adults had grown up there.

Most evenings after dinner we were confined to the living room since my early to bed and early to rise father insisted on lights out by eight o'clock. Because the configuration of the house followed most old Santa Fe homes, having started with one room and others added as time went by, we had to walk through their bedroom to get to the bathroom or the kitchen. There were no doorways, just archways between the rooms, so it was imperative that we keep noise to a minimum so as not to wake my parents. We kept the volume on the outdated television so low we could barely hear what was going on.

In *Lowrider Blues*, I included this observation about my childhood home:

"I grew up in a house without hallways. No wide halls to walk down holding your arms out like an angel whose wings whisked against the walls dislodging tiny fragments of dust. No hallways that separated rooms which could be closed off by a wooden door, where private thoughts could be thought and clutter could be hidden from view. No rooms which could be darkened by closed doors and drawn curtains, blocking off any hint of daylight. No rooms in which a tired or lonely body could sleep until forever. In our house, we were welcome in every room. We walked from room to room without the need of hallways, rooms which had no doors, only archways to separate them. Archways which would pass the light from room to room, with added light coming from transparent panels hidden under heavy curtains pulled together only at night.

"You couldn't run and hide in our house, except maybe in the bathroom which had a door, or the living room/bedroom, which also had a door. But neither of these rooms were available full time for hiding or crying. I wonder if the hallways would have made a difference in separating us from each other. Would we have been less inclined to wonder what was wrong if we couldn't see the fearful looks or the red eyes; if we couldn't hear the painful sighs, the nighttime sobs or early morning laughter?

"Our house was built without an architect, without a blueprint, with only a drawing in the dirt made with a stick. It was a rectangular adobe box with four rooms of almost equal size, with rounded archways in between to keep life flowing through from room to room. Yes, we had no hallways to run down holding our arms out like angel wings; but we had a house where life lived." Excerpted from *Lowrider Blues*, Sunstone Press.2009

Before long, I was fortunate to find a job at a downtown law firm and after my first couple of paychecks we moved into an apartment house about two miles south of my old neighborhood.

Our first night there, the kids stayed up past midnight, munching on popcorn and watching television, a luxury they had previously gone without. After a time, I went on a few dates, but nothing serious; nothing sleeping-over worthy. Then I met someone in a bar. (Sound familiar?)

I was thirty-three years old and bored of spending nights and weekends at home with nothing to do but laundry and housework. Mother watched the kids while I went out. I didn't deliberately end up in a bar, though. It was 1975 and on my birthday that year, my brother invited me to watch *the game* at Ramon's Lounge, a popular hangout for blue and other color collar workers. It was Super Bowl IX weekend and Terry Bradshaw and the Pittsburgh Steelers were about to do battle against the Minnesota Vikings. Everyone in the bar cheered as the two teams dubbed the Steel Curtain and Purple People Eaters took the field. Up to that point in time my life had not included sports, either by active participation or as part of the television audience. I didn't know the difference between a nine iron and a hockey puck. When I was in California tracking the last knight, we attended game three of the World Series where the Oakland Athletics defeated the Los Angeles Dodgers. This Super Bowl game provided a similar veil of boredom, which I hid by faking my enthusiasm as the crowd cheered. I couldn't wait for it to be over.

My brother Jimmy sat at a booth with a couple of barflies, for lack of a better description, so I sidled in next to him and ordered a ginger ale. As I sipped on my third soft drink, a thirty-something guy meandered over to our table to chat with my brother. He was dressed in Wranglers, boots and a cowboy shirt that set off his turquoise blue eyes. He was of average height and had a trim physique. I noted he was mildly handsome in a rugged sort of way, his skin bronzed from the southwestern sun. He was also mostly drunk, and I would discover later he was also mostly married, but almost out the door on that one. He offered his hand and remarked that I was really a "sweet thing" and he was happy to make my acquaintance. He hung around during half-time and returned to wherever he was sitting at the bar to finish off the fresh rum and Coke the bartender set in front of him. Every time I looked up, I caught his glazed-over eyes staring in my direction, accompanied by a seductive wink. I could feel the blush on my cheeks even in the dim light of the lounge.

My brother was engrossed in his own attempt to score on a woman wearing a dress so high above her knees it left nothing to the imagination. I was feeling like a third wheel, so I forced a smile and turned my head, pretending to be interested in the half-time presentation on the mega screens surrounding the bar. The cowboy staggered over and squeezed in next to me. I looked at my brother, hoping he would discourage the man, but he said it wasn't going to kill me to sit with the guy for a few minutes. So off I went, feeling as though I was being led to the gallows. When I looked back, my brother and the girl in the miniskirt were headed for the exit.

For months I had experienced a continual state of stress and exhaustion from holding down a job and seeing to my children's needs. There weren't enough hours in the evenings and weekends to not only keep up the house and laundry, but to provide what meager entertainment I could afford. Cleaning up involved mostly shoving all the clutter into the nearest closet, a habit I suspect my daughters still practice. I wasn't yet receiving child support, so everything continued to fall on my shoulders, and I was feeling the heavy burden of it all. At least that was my excuse for cultivating a relationship that I should have vetoed when the fictional vote came up.

The blue-eyed cowboy I met on Super Bowl weekend called one evening. I was flattered by the attention of a man I perceived had a gentle soul. It wasn't long before he moved into our small apartment and life instantly became easier. He was gainfully employed and earned a decent salary as an electrician and without hesitation began to contribute generously to our monthly expenses. Initially, my father wasn't too keen on my becoming involved again, particularly with this man whose family history he was familiar with. During the 1950s, the cowboy's grandmother owned a bar and a cathouse on Canyon Road in Santa Fe and currently resided at her 3500-acre ranch in Cerrillos, NM. As far as my father was concerned, she did not have a very good reputation since rumors still circulated that she continued to be the madam of a profitable service. She was also mean enough to shoot anyone who wandered onto the Indian ruins on her property. The only saving grace he considered a good point about D was that he was a blue-collar worker and a member of a labor union, as my father and brothers had been for the better part of their lives.

In mid-summer of 1975, we traveled to Mexico with a group of his friends, which included my brother and his girlfriend. We lounged around the heated pool at La Quinta Inn in Ciudad Juarez and enjoyed sumptuous meals at a fraction of the cost back home. We wandered through the busy marketplace looking for Talavera pottery and bottles of Kahlua to take across the border and watched greyhound dog races at the Hipodromo Juarez racetrack. The weather was perfect, the hotel was first class, and at sundown we returned to sit at the bar, with patrons dancing to the music and drinking margaritas. Sometime on the spur of the moment before we were to return home, D suggested we should get married. No, he didn't get down on one knee or profess his undying love by shouting from the rooftops. It was more in the way of a casual comment. Not one to pass up a semi-legitimate marriage proposal, I said yes.

We gathered up my brother and his girlfriend and found a *Justicia de la Paz.* Once inside, we showed the clerk our IDs and waited about an hour on wood benches in a long hallway, and then we were herded into a mid-sized room where a portly man with a handlebar moustache sat behind a worn desk. On the wall behind him was a large wood replica of the Mexican seal. He shuffled a few papers on the desk, stood and walked us over to a corner of the room and directed us to stand in the center of a rickety arbor replete with plastic flowers and doves. He smiled broadly and uttered a few sentences in Spanglish, pronounced us *esposo* and *esposa* and that was it. He walked back to the desk, stamped a seal on the certificate and the assistant with an equally minimal grasp of the English language directed us to the exit where she handed us an envelope with the marriage certificate.

Moving forward, I had not yet had a successful marriage and I hoped that weekend in Juarez would provide a new beginning. When we returned to Santa Fe, my children did not care to live in his modern double-wide trailer parked at a lot on Airport Road on the outskirts of Santa Fe, more than ten miles from downtown. This would have put them into one of the lesser school districts and I would have to drive them there every day. I wasn't too crazy about trailer life myself, finding it surreal to be living in the middle of rows of varying sizes of mobile homes with few walls, fences or gardens separating them. To remedy this situation, before the end of summer I sold my secretarial service and garnered sufficient funds for a down payment on a house in the newly expanded Bellamah area with a more desirable school district one block directly east of busy Cerrillos Road. So, in a few short years I had married cowboys and Indians, both ends of the spectrum. This one had worn many hats in his lifetime: a steer-roping cowboy, a bucking bronc rider, a dyed in the wool cattle rancher, a yippie-hi-yo kind of guy who could also drink anyone under the table. He was a country music loving dancing fool who could waltz across Texas and two-step right into your heart. I believed there was a sweetheart of a man waiting to emerge from behind door number three, and I was willing to make that choice. I figured I could deal with his drinking. After all, I grew up with it . . . how bad could it be?

He had nothing to hide and repeated more than once: *I enjoy drinking; I will not stop drinking for you, my grandmother, or my dead mother. I was a drinker when you met me.* I was undaunted by these words and was in hearing mode but not listening mode. I would go on to ignore every red-flagged incident that popped up over time because I was Wonder Woman and my magic bracelets contained superpowers. I *could* change him. Just watch me. Eat my dust. For seventeen years I would eat more than dust; I would not only eat my own words, but I would choke on them. There did not exist a power great enough to deter this man from his path. He was bound and determined (albeit subconsciously) to drink himself to death or die trying. He had set his sights years before we met, and I came along believing I could fix him. *I wasn't able to fix me and I didn't even know I needed fixing.* Like a child determined to outsmart a bully, I overlooked the chaos in our household, while I angrily emptied quarts of expensive rum into the sink. There in the back of my mind was the perceived solution, so flawed it is worth another mention: *I believed everything would be fine in the morning. My grandmother had believed it, my mother had believed it, and without hesitation, I believed it.*

25 | IN THE EYE OF THE HURRICANE

IT WAS EARLY MORNING AS I CRACKED MY EYES OPEN and looked around the unfamiliar surroundings. Across the room I saw a closet filled from top to bottom with neatly stacked boxes of size seven women's shoes. Momentarily disoriented, I had forgotten we were at my friend Jenny's house on the west side of Santa Fe. I looked over to see my children snuggled together on a mattress on the floor, sleeping the slumber of angels. We came to Jenny's house the evening before because D was more inebriated than usual, raising more hell than usual, and being more verbally abusive than usual. It wasn't worth remembering what he was hollering about this time, but it usually involved his own demons: suspicion, insecurity and insane jealousy.

One evening the prior week, he had been hollering at the top of his lungs, accusing me of sleeping with everyone and their brother or some other imaginary infidelity. Over the years I learned to zone him out, probably much like my mother did when my father began his rants. Always in perpetual pacifier mode, I offered to reheat dinner, even if it was long past time. In one swift motion he grabbed the overflowing bowl of spaghetti and flung it into the wall, sending pieces of the ceramic bowl flying in all directions as the noodles and sauce momentarily clung to the Cobalt blue

Talavera tiles on the wall before they slithered to the floor in slow motion. The next morning, I dutifully cleaned up the mess, after which I went to wake the children for school. My nine-year-old daughter was not in her room, nor anywhere in the house. In a panic I woke the other two. The eight-year-old said that when D wouldn't stop hollering, her sister climbed out the window and ran to the Franciscan nuns' house at the end of the street. I reached for a sweater and hurried down the street, embarrassed to knock on their door. I was unsure what to say, but with downcast eyes I thanked them and walked her home, grateful she hadn't gone any farther and was safe. Looking back, I would venture a guess that incidents such as this are the reason that daughter has had a lifetime of difficult relationships. (I have learned that as parents we can observe and express our concern but can do nothing about the path each child has chosen in adulthood.)

And now, the previous night when I saw the fear in my children's eyes, I gathered them up and left, telling D enough was enough. But *enough* was never *enough*. There were degrees of enough: Not enough, just enough, just a little more, one more time. I usually gave him more rope than I got, but hey, I figured that was compromise. Wasn't that what marriage is about? Wasn't that what women were expected to do for their man? I either sat silent or vigorously participated in inane arguments about nothing, spurred on by his having gone far beyond the limits of alcohol consumption and my having reached my own limits of tolerance yet one more time. *Was it so wrong of me to want love, romance, security? Or was it all a pipe dream conjured up by a part of me that didn't have a grasp on the nature of reality. I had been searching for someone to love me, and at that moment I didn't even like myself.* I failed to recognize my own life might be out of control and I might be experiencing just a tad of denial. Not much. Just a tad. Already at my wit's end, earlier in the marriage I scheduled an appointment with Shanti, a German psychologist who practiced in a nearby town. Half hour into our third session, she told me of her concern that this man might harm me, considering his alcoholic rages. Without hesitation I responded that was the farthest thing from my mind; that he was a good man (sober). At least that was the fallacy with which I assuaged myself.

My children and I stayed an additional couple of days at my friend's small house, and not wanting to overstay our welcome, decided we had been gone long enough for things to cool down and it was safe to go home. That evening I circled our neighborhood and the front of our house, checking to see if his truck was nearby. It wasn't. I parked in the driveway, gathered up the children, blankets and stuffed animals and headed for the door. From the street I could see that every light in the house was on and as we entered through the garage the kids let out a combined gasp. I rushed into the family room to see what their panicked cries were about. The massive custom brick fireplace constructed during a recent remodeling had been completely destroyed and white brick chunks were scattered all over the carpet. The walls in the living room and hallway all had gaping holes. The windows in the children's rooms had been shattered and the walls smashed in. My son's room received the brunt of the damage, the psychological impact of which would surface years later. As word of the damage spread to D's barroom friends, they admiringly nicknamed him *Sledge.* I would imagine that when he heard this, a sly smile formed on his lips as he nudged closer to the bar and cradled a cocktail in his hands. This spoke not only for his character but that of his acquaintances, to be of the mindset that destroying a home deserved pats on the back and a descriptive moniker.

An event as horrific as this surely should have heralded the end of the relationship, the total deterioration of any hope that might have existed. For the ensuing months I oversaw the reconstruction of the interior of the house which fortunately was covered by insurance. Although I knew it, I couldn't prove that D had been the perpetrator and unless I filed charges against him, the underwriter determined it was vandalism and paid for the repairs. The bricklayer shook his head in dismay as he observed the damage inflicted to his original handiwork by his maniacal sledgehammer-wielding friend. We stayed apart during those months and interacted very little. I continued to work, the kids continued to attend school and we settled into life as it was. To keep my mind occupied I focused on creating art projects and through a grant from the National Endowment for the Arts undertook the task of documenting my parents' tinwork process and designs. This involved sketching templates of their patterns and photographing the finished product. During those days I was more relaxed, my children appeared more content without the resident bogeyman and life continued on.

Eventually he started coming by, at first to make sure I had enough money to cover the bills and that our pantry was sufficiently stocked. In a remorseful state filled with apologies and assurances, he said he had stopped drinking and couldn't bear to live without us any longer and would I consider taking him back. All right, so by now you know I'm a sucker for a good sob-story, particularly one accompanied by tears and promises of redemption. We reconciled and set about regluing the pieces of our lives together. It wasn't long before a house came up for sale around the corner from my old neighborhood in the South Capitol area. The house where we lived contained too many bad memories and even though they had been covered over with layers of fresh plaster, I could still imagine the holes in the wall and I'm sure my children were also able to do this.

It was 1978, three years into marriage, and my children were attending Wood-Gormley School, the same elementary school I attended as a child thirty years before. I no longer was required to make the twenty-mile round trip from the previous house to check on my parents each day; life was good. Although I still worked at a downtown law firm, I was beginning to spend more time cultivating my creative talents at the encouragement of my parents. I was helping them sell their wares at the annual Spanish Market in downtown Santa Fe, and much of my art was selling like hotcakes. Added to this, D continued to bring in a substantial paycheck as an electrical foreman for a contract company in Los Alamos.

Although he had never completely stopped drinking, at least he was civil most of the time; the rest of the time I did the usual and ignored him. He never drank alcohol before evening, which I rationalized was a good point and showed that at least he had some self-control where drinking was concerned. As part of his self-prescribed penance, he set about to convert the garage, added the necessary accoutrements to make it workable, and voila, I now had a large studio with the necessary equipment and tools to become a woodcarver and pursue the art of the 19th century saint makers. I continued to work part-time at home as a legal transcriber, which gave me time to pursue my artistic endeavors. My existence became tolerable with few disruptive incidents. I was slowly falling in love again, this time with creating art.

26 | GUESS WHAT'S IN THE OVEN

In 1983 I was forty-one and a full-time artist completely enmeshed as a *Santera* (saint-maker) in creating traditional New Mexican religious art, by then having participated for several years in Spanish Market. Just when things were starting to look up and I was spending more time perfecting my artistic style, my seventeen-year-old daughter showed up pregnant. We learned of her predicament from a school counselor who called to inquire if we were aware of this. A few months previously she had chosen to leave home rather than live under our house rules. We also discovered that she had quit school and was living in a wigwam (not a tent) somewhere on private property and sleeping on the dirt floor. We tracked her down and after a long discussion, agreed to allow her to return home. After all, that was no place for a pregnant teen, even if she thought nothing of it.

From that day on, my daughter held the bathroom hostage, priming and primping for hours at a time and then leaving a mess for someone else to pick up, water trickling and blow dryers and curling irons still connected. As she entered her fifth month, she had become lazy, hostile and uncooperative, with no consideration for her siblings, whom she often bullied. Because of her disruptive nature, and that our health insurance wouldn't cover teenage pregnancies, I arranged for her to spend the remainder of the pregnancy at a home for unwed mothers in Albuquerque. Once the child was born, this step would pave the way for her to receive assistance from the State. She required the kind of help I couldn't provide and having her there was a temporary Band-Aid to my keeping a grip on my sanity and a bit of peace in the family. It was near impossible to function with her around, although arranging this would turn out to be a subconscious grudge she would carry into her adult life and bring it up whenever the opportunity arose.

Shortly after my grandson's birth, we noticed that motherhood didn't come easily for her. She was still young and wanted to go out dancing and hanging out with her same-aged friends. Sometimes that night out would extend for as much as a week, while I cared for the infant, wondering where she was. Eventually he came to live with us full time. It wasn't an easy task to rearrange our lives to accommodate the little auburn-headed ball of energy, but at least for a while it seemed to add a much-needed dimension missing from our relationship. Always determined to retain the upper hand, she would not allow us to adopt him, but agreed to guardianship instead, limited to us providing schooling and his inclusion on our health insurance policy. Through a series of attorney visits, we discovered then that grandparents had few or no rights.

Like many unhappy housewives, I turned to food for comfort. During my daughter's pregnancy, I experienced a slow and subtle weight gain while indulging in an assortment of comfort foods. My weight reflected the condition of my life. Oh, I didn't balloon up overnight, but gradually gained thirty pounds of padding so the vile words D regularly flung in my direction could easily bounce off. I had convinced myself that everything he said was true, and each time I looked in the mirror, the reflection that stared back at me reinforced the belief that I was fat and unattractive, and nobody would ever want me. (Never mind that by all standards I was merely overweight, perhaps pleasingly plump rather than obese.)

True to nature, he never remembered much the morning after over-indulgence, but I did. The memory was stored deep within the crevices of both my mind and body. In between taking care of my two teenagers still at home, the new addition to our family and working in my studio, I continued to look for emotional comfort. D had always loved to cook and during our marriage he pan-fried just about everything. Weekend breakfasts consisted of home-made hash-brown potatoes, bacon, eggs, biscuits and cream gravy. On a weekly basis we consumed grilled Porterhouse steaks, baked potatoes with butter and sour cream, tossed salads dredged with home-made ranch dressing, and nachos layered with gobs of cheese and jalapeno peppers. I could sit through an entire football game and never watch a minute of it. I was the great pretender. *Anything to maintain the status quo.* When it was my turn to cook, I filled our table with foods from my childhood, beans, tortillas, enchiladas, tacos, red and green chile and fluffy sopaipillas filled with potatoes, meat and cheese.

Since eating habits were developed in childhood, I recalled how much my father liked avocados. He would slit one in half, remove the seed and fill the center with mayonnaise and then spoon out the contents, mouthful by mouthful. He was also fond of goat cheese, buttermilk, and baked bread. I would like to be able to say that during my childhood eating was ceremonial, ritualistic. But it wasn't. Eating filled one of the cavernous gaps in my existence. I had grown up with the typical foods of a Hispano neighborhood. I looked forward to each meal that served as a substitute for love. As our relationship waxed and waned, family dinners became scarcer. The dinner meal now consisted of pizza, burgers, chicken tenders and other fast food readily available on Santa Fe's main drag. As luck would have it, whenever we ordered fast food, more often than not D's order would either be missing or incomplete. He would then have an excuse to throw a bloody fit and deliberately toss his meal into the trash, while we looked on with dropped jaws in anticipation of the explosion that would surely follow. The enjoyment of sharing a McDonald's Happy Meal was definitely sucked out of the air by yet another senseless tirade.

My grandson was the light of my life then and is still special in my books. He was loving and funny, taking delight in working next to me in my studio. He inherited a creative streak and by the time he was five he was painting small wooden retablos with quaint figures gleaned from biblical stories. He was a tiny artist in the making, and the glue holding my emotions together. He entered Spanish Market when he was five and participated until he was seventeen. After giving her second child up for adoption, my daughter went on to marry the father of her next three children and I continued to raise the first one.

Even though it would have been in the better interests of my grandson, she continued to block our efforts to adopt him; instead after twelve years went by, she would claim ownership of him by showing up at his school and taking possession as though he was a pet kitten. When she went to the school office, they would not let her take him because she was not on their list. Undaunted, she snuck up the back stairs and removed him from the classroom. In my mind, the purpose of this "kidnapping" was that he was then old enough to babysit her three additional children, not taking into consideration that he was comfortable living with me. This was a traumatic experience for not only my grandson, but for me as well. He was brainwashed into believing I didn't want him and that he was better off with them, a fact I would become aware of years later in one of our intimate conversations about his life and the damage inflicted to his psyche by being pulled out of the life he had known for over a decade. To prove that I was unfit to care for him, she hired a "therapist" and provided her with a twisted narrative, alleging that I expressed I was in a new relationship and needed my space. Ensuing visits with him were restricted and if I did not return him at the specified time, she threatened to call the Sheriff. I now know why he was so uncomfortable during our visits, it having been pounded into his head that I no longer wanted him in my life.

The up and down relationship with my first-born daughter has remained strained to this day, no matter how much effort I exert to assuage the wounds she silently alludes to when things don't go her way. Not everyone is comfortable on a therapist's couch spilling their guts out truthfully. I continue to wish her well in her life as I seek remedies to come to terms with my own life and repair the damage done to my grandson, who is now in his late thirties. He listened to the lies they told the therapist and has retained unhappy memories of that period in his life, never having been given the opportunity to sit down with his birth mother and discuss his feelings. Fortunately, they gave him up a couple of years later and allowed him to come back to me, but the damage had been done. Thankfully my son enrolled him at the local prep school and he was able to obtain a decent education from junior high on.

27 | RIDE 'EM, COWBOY

SOMETIME BEFORE THE COMPLETE DEMISE of our marriage, D received an invitation in the mail to a *Stomper* reunion with many of his high school buddies. In mid-1950s Santa Fe, stompers were *cowboys,* both wannabe and genuine, all decked out in Levi and Wrangler jeans, topped with colorful western shirts decorated with faux-pearl buttons, and boots made from exotic leathers on those from more affluent families. During his own lifetime, D had lived as a cowboy, who not only rode bucking broncs but spent most of his childhood herding and branding cattle on his grandmother's 3500-acre ranch in Cerrillos, twenty miles southeast of Santa Fe. The reunion took place at the home of a stomper girl he had known since grade school and who had been one of my junior high through high school classmates. That night he didn't return home. I was accustomed to him staying out late at the bar, but this was different. I wasn't sure if I should consider that he might be lying dead in an arroyo somewhere, or if there was a reasonable explanation. There was, and I wasn't going to like it. At noon the next day, his story was that he arrived at the reunion with every intention of just having a few beers and catching up with his old buddies. Then after consuming a six-pack or so of beer, he ran into Barbara, the girl who had been his first true love in high school and the one who had rejected his proposal of marriage. Just to spite her and hide his disappointment, he went on to marry and have two children with his second choice, the 1958 Santa Fe Rodeo Queen, who did say yes.

About a year before this reunion took place, I read a book by Louise Hay on the subject of creative visualization and how one could manifest events just by putting the concept out into the universe. I thought it was a novel idea for the times that maybe if D met someone else, they would go off together and I would be free to pursue my own life, whatever that might have been at the time. I tried to visualize what this person would look and act like. I figured young and perky with ponytailed blonde hair, tight jeans and a cowboy shirt, and they would dance off into the sunset never to be seen again. Believing that such an effort might work, I presented the image to the universe on a regular basis, writing affirmations in a yellow tablet, filling page after page, and then at some point setting that tedious practice aside. Well, to my surprise, there she was, folks. She was neither blonde and perky nor young, but no matter.

D stood next to our kitchen table, puffed out his chest and informed me he was leaving and intended to pursue the relationship he never had with Barb. What a turn of events this was—talk about being able to manifest a situation more or less as you imagined it. It was obvious Louise Hay knew what she was talking about—or was it a huge coincidence? Within weeks, the new couple traveled to Oklahoma, and once there, loaded up a U-Haul trailer and transported her belongings back to Santa Fe. They set up housekeeping at a condo on the north side of town, and there I stood, in shock at how quickly my life had changed. Yes, I had dreamed of him leaving; and yes, I wanted to get out of the relationship, but obviously I didn't want it badly enough.

My grandson and I were now living alone, and I was having a difficult time explaining to a four-year-old why his Poppa wasn't there anymore. I was also feeling a bit indignant that he had the audacity to end our relationship without even a fight. Yes, yes, I know. In disguise, it was a dream come true. I should have taken that opportunity and run with it. But I wasn't finished yet. How did I feel when he hooked up with the high school sweetheart he hadn't seen for over thirty years? The tango of *I really didn't want him, but I also didn't want anyone else to have him* came into play. Of course, I wanted out of this relationship, but a part of me wasn't ready for him to experience one single moment of happiness . . . no siree, I wasn't giving up that easily. This would have been the perfect opportunity to get out of a repressive relationship; instead, my own pile of insecurities took the wheel and I felt threatened. Why should he be happy and I miserable?

Several months later he stopped by for a visit, once again to make sure I was able to keep up expenses. As we sat across from each other in my studio after small talking for a few minutes, he admitted he had made a mistake. He missed my grandson and was feeling a little sheepish that he had gone through all the trouble of getting this woman moved here from Oklahoma and then discovering they had little in common after all these years (other than smoking and drinking, I imagined). He was caught up in the notion of who they had been, not who they were. He solemnly promised me that if I took him back, he would start attending AA meetings and maybe work out the problems I had with his drinking. (Had I not heard this somewhere in the past-- promises of redemption?) It did sound too good to be true, but I was willing to take the chance of perhaps making another go of it. By then, all three of my children had left the nest, were out on their own, and I was in my mid-forties. A new beginning might just be what the doctor ordered. I felt sorry for Babs and couldn't imagine her humiliation, but hey, all's fair in love and war, isn't it? I'm sure it didn't seem that way to her as she stood in the U-Haul kiosk to rent a truck and gather up her belongings and head back to Oklahoma.

No matter how much I hoped he would finally begin to exhibit a knightly demeanor, I quickly learned that you really couldn't fashion a silk purse from a sow's ear. As artistically creative I had become, I couldn't make a sober man from an inebriated one; I couldn't tap the heels of my ruby slippers together and make wishes come true, and try as I might, I couldn't obtain a heart for the tin man. I was still the cowardly lion hoping to develop enough courage to leave the marriage and get a life.

After seventeen years of a tumultuous relationship, I filed for divorce. No point in elaborating, but he really put the screws to me, picking far more nits than were necessary. He had the advantage of having settled his grandmother's estate with my help some years before and could afford a high-powered attorney. Together they backed me up against a wall. I was required to either sell the house or pay him half the equity in cash. In the next week I sold my Spanish Colonial art collection and submitted the proceeds to his attorney. He then agreed the balance could be paid off by one-third of my earnings for the next five years. He retained his IBEW union benefits. To make matters worse, he ultimately purchased a house on our same street, rationalizing that he needed to stay in the area because of the tinwork business he had developed. It was a little too close for my liking, as I had surmised, he could observe my every move from his front porch, which he did.

28 | RETURN TO THE SHADOWS

BY THE TIME THE MARRIAGE HAD MOVED TOWARD its eventual and complete collapse, I was convinced I was fat, unattractive, worthless, and incapable of survival without him, and that no other man would want me. He had repeated these statements often enough and my subconscious believed every word. After the divorce, an entire year passed and the truth of his prophecy became even more apparent. I went on only one date that year, and I did the asking, to a gathering at the Stanley Marcus residence, accompanied by a man who had attended one of the classes I taught. And that was it. I never had another date, not even an invitation, so I concluded my ex-husband had obviously been right. As the year drew toward winter, we reconciled, mostly through my efforts. The overwhelming loneliness and insecurity blocked out whatever common sense might have remained. This cowardly lion's new courage hadn't lasted very long.

I soon discovered he had changed considerably in that year apart, unfortunately not for the better. He hadn't let any grass grow under his feet and had become a dues-paying card-carrying member of the Fraternal Order of Eagles, an organization whose Santa Fe members spent much of their free time sitting at a long bar, drinking into the wee hours of the morning. At this club, newly single men, particularly those who were financially secure, were a premium catch for the unhappy divorcees and regular barflies who hung out at the bar at all hours. I don't know if this was universally true at all fraternal organizations, but it certainly was true of this one. Women seemed to come out of the woodwork, and every man was fair game as long as free drinks kept flowing. D relished in the attention showered on him and it made him conceited and cocky, an unbecoming state for this cowboy.

In the early spring we signed up for a two-week trip to London and Rome with members of the local Catholic and Episcopal churches, the farthest distance I had ever traveled in my life. Because of residual damage to my middle ear from a virus the previous year, I was apprehensive about making such a long trip, a nine-hour flight from Baltimore. In a continuous state of anxiety, once we boarded the Alitalia 747, I must have recited a hundred rosaries and listened to my relaxation cassette tape fifty times, while D siphoned cocktails provided by the attractive stewardess, and he slept the excess hours away while I continued my silent prayers.

Safe on the ground in Rome, we took a bus from the airport to a quaint hotel a few blocks from the Vatican. Early the next morning after a breakfast of baguettes, butter, jam and dark coffee, we were herded into the tour bus to take us to the quaint village of Assisi to visit the Basilica of St. Francis, where Father Jerome, our accompanying priest, conducted a mass in the chapel which housed the venerated saint's tomb. That moment was a spiritual experience for all those in attendance. I saw tears form in D's eyes and wondered what he was thinking at the time. The momentary impact diminished by sunset. I have no doubt that in his own way he did enjoy himself for most of the trip but out of habit, I still walked on eggshells even on the cobblestoned streets of Rome as we headed to partake of the magnificent art housed in the Vatican which we had only seen in magazines or PBS specials.

Each evening as his drinking reached its usual maximum level, the magnificence of the sights we visited were overshadowed by slurred conversation and cutting remarks. He balked at my requests to take it easy, since we were in the presence of all the Catholics and Episcopalians from our group, and I was embarrassed by his demeanor. I learned a valuable lesson from that trip. Never travel with an individual who has no common sense or dignity when drunk. Our visit to the Vatican, being within touching distance of Pope John Paul, and masses at Assisi and St. Peter's Cathedral, the beautiful churches, historic architecture, gardens and art were all diminished by his constant haranguing and belittlement once evening drew to a close.

After a week in Rome, we flew to England, landed at Heathrow airport and immediately boarded a tour bus, then traveled some 250 miles to Jarrow, to visit the birthplace of St. Bede, the patron saint of the Episcopal group with whom we traveled. After stopping for Evensong at several English cathedrals on the return trip, we spent the remainder of the afternoon at Westminster Cathedral, in time to catch the Evensong presentation there. I preferred the cathedrals of Rome, with the architecture and ancient art, compared to the sameness of the English churches, but there was a quietude present in those magnificent buildings. Back in London, we were fortunate to witness a lavish parade of English royalty stemming from Buckingham Palace. Nutcracker soldiers and fairy tale sights filled the streets where crowds cheered and hailed Queen Elizabeth and her entourage.

As far as D's drinking, London was not much different, other than more ale, less wine and an interesting fish and chips experience. I had heard much about fish and chips, so I imagined crispy pieces of battered fish served with French fries. Instead, the meal consisted of greasy portions of both served on brown paper. To add to my concerns, on our last day in London I began to experience mild vertigo-like symptoms which threw me off balance. I was anxious that this might continue through our return trip to the states. In search of an acupuncturist who might provide some relief, we inquired of several locals then trekked many miles through the city, discovering that the "short way" in the directions we were given was a very long distance. Having received treatment, we returned to the hotel, exhausted. Where was a London cabbie when you needed them. The following day we returned to Rome, gathered our belongings, and boarded the Alitalia white-knuckle flight home. The most difficult portion of the trip was the turbulent weather which surfaced as we departed from Denver and I held on tight to the arm rests as the plane rocked and rolled through the torrential winds and rain which followed us all the way to Albuquerque. I had never been so happy to set foot on Mother Earth.

After the trip, It took only a few months for me to come to terms and admit I had made a serious mistake by being foolish enough to pursue yet another reconciliation. There wasn't much of a home life, as after we returned from our trip, most of our time was spent hanging out at the club, primarily him drinking and commiserating with his friends, and me standing by the wayside pretending to enjoy myself.

At the end of that year, I knew we had spent our last Christmas together, but it was obvious he didn't. He still entertained some kind of warped hope that we could continue the charade. Under the tree was a Rolex watch, a gift I wanted to someday be able to purchase for myself to represent my success as an artist. I was developing a following in traditional art circles and had completed several large commissions for historic churches in northern New Mexico. In addition, since the mid-1980s I had become a dealer in antique Spanish Colonial art and my expertise in the field had developed into a lucrative side career, creating an additional source of income. My colleague for a number of years was a handsome Argentinian named Carlos, with whom I developed a close personal and business relationship which has continued over the years. He plied me with his vast knowledge of everything Spanish Colonial and I educated him in my field. We were successful in locating many examples of this art and reselling them at escalated prices, as these old santos and tinwork were now in great demand by collectors.

Slowly, my marriage continued to erode and turn ugly. I could no longer tune out his drunken rants during which he would become enraged if I attempted to close the kitchen window so the next-door neighbors couldn't hear his loud outbursts peppered with vile words and accusations. It was no longer enough for me to make some flip remark about the circumstances and walk away. He was frustrated and angry and determined that everything was my fault. He had agreed to reconcile believing I would not break his heart again and that we could eventually work things out, although he put little effort into making any substantive changes. It was as though he felt his presence in my life was enough, something which was no longer true.

In the months prior to the divorce, he had taken early retirement from his job in Los Alamos, and we were thrown together for a much greater time than before. By helping my parents take care of their overflow, he perfected his own craft of tin-smithing and formed a small cottage industry of his own, much as my parents had, and much to the chagrin of my tinsmith brothers, who felt that as an Anglo he had no right to do so. Since my studio was a converted two-car garage, there was ample space for more than one artist. Creating functional pieces of art out of sheets of tin was noisy and disturbing to me and was one of the reasons I had never followed in my parents' footsteps and chose carving and painting instead. My only solace during this period came from my grandson and working in my half of the studio, where nothing could penetrate the shield of tranquility I erected around myself as I worked diligently with my hands and heart to create religious paintings and traditional wood sculptures for upcoming markets. That peace continues to fuel me to this day.

Do I look back and wonder how much fault I had in the deterioration of the relationship? Do I wonder if I had lessened my insistence on his attaining sobriety and just let him be would things have been different? Perhaps, but probably not. At my father's funeral in 1998, I realized how deep D's anger and resentment toward me still remained. After the service I reached out to thank him for coming and he turned his back to me.

29 | I WISH I HAD A CRYSTAL BALL

Sometime in the mid-1990s I browsed through a New Age store at the mouth of Canyon Road in Santa Fe, hoping to find a relaxation tape for my cassette player, similar to the one that had seen me through the trip to Italy. My stress level hadn't diminished much over the years, and I relied on these recordings to alleviate some of the daily dung I was shoveling through. I had never been in a shop with so many unusual items, and hundreds of quartz crystals suspended from the ceiling of the main room. I had read books about visualization and manifestation, and had even listened to Tony Robbins, so it wasn't a stretch for me to be curious about self-help books and philosophy. As I skimmed through the cassette tape section, I stumbled on a conversation between two women, one of whom I learned was a psychic and a channeler of some wise entity somewhere off in the universe. I couldn't even pretend to understand what a psychic medium did, but I could see that her customers appeared to be interested (if not enchanted) by what she had to say.

I paid for my tape and the clerk said I could have a free reading if I liked. My parents would have dragged me out of there before I had a chance to respond. Their culture (and religion) did not allow a belief in fortune tellers, not even for entertainment.

But what the heck, I was fifty years old and it would be a first for me. I seated myself at the table next to the psychic and listened to what wisdom she had to impart. Impressionable as I tended to be, I found most of her predictions to be right on. She pretty much said everything I wanted to hear. Not only was I going to be the recipient of a financial windfall, but I was also going to find the romance I had been searching for, and even marriage was in the future. Wow, and this was just a free short reading. Imagine how much information I could gain if I made an appointment for a full reading. So, I did just that.

During that period of my life, I was not interested in an emotional or spiritual *awakening*. I'm not sure if those words were even a part of my vocabulary. I just wanted to be happy, and isn't that what happens when you see the knight approaching over the horizon? Over the next six months I sat through several *readings*, coupled with several deep regressions into past lives to try to determine the reason for some of my health issues. During one session it appeared I had watched a young relative drown in the river and couldn't help them for fear of drowning myself (thus my fear of water). In another, my frontier husband had left me alone to die of influenza while he went off hunting. Believe it or not, during that time we ran a general store and in my mind's eye I could see the rows of sugar sacks and different barrels of provisions stacked on the shelves. A later regression involved being held captive in a medieval castle and accosted by a lesbian soldier who resembled Joan of Arc. The psychic was either very good at what she did, or I had an imaginative and fruitful (not to mention overactive) mind. Eventually I tired of the sameness of the readings and realized that most of what she predicted never really came true. My every desire was probably written all over my face and easily transmittable.

Would I ever find the kind of love that would make up for every unkind word that had ever been uttered at me? I doubted it then. I realize now that my childhood had been one protracted anxiety attack, but I didn't know what that meant. Outwardly I believed I was thoughtful, helpful, friendly, always willing to please. Inwardly I was needy, fearful, and terrified of being abandoned. I wonder if anyone (including myself) ever noticed that about me. Did I just utter the words in conversations to be accepted or did I mean them; and if there was a response, was it just an echo of my own thoughts? Why was it so easy to live a lifelong lie, pretending to have it all together; when underneath a different, frightened person existed? Could it be that I had dual personalities, one hiding the other? I know I ask a lot of questions, but that's because I sure would like a lot of answers.

Still searching outside of myself for answers, I happened upon a Yoga studio across from Trader Joe's, and I periodically glanced into the window as I passed the building. I had occasionally skimmed past an early morning PBS Lilias Yoga program, but never quite knew what yoga was about. So, I ventured into this sparkly clean section of the strip mall next to Subway and was greeted by a tiny Korean woman wearing a white belted outfit much like those seen in the Karate Kid. She handed me a couple of pamphlets and said I could come for a sample lesson and scheduled me for the next day. I showed up and was directed to a large room to wait for other students. The group was required to bow to a gilt-framed photograph of the "leader," a handsome Korean man who appeared to be in his late thirties. Each day students were led through a series of stretches and movements, ending with joyfully letting go and dancing around like children. This was followed by a tea ceremony and a sharing circle where we were all seated cross-legged on the floor and asked to reveal some aspect of our lives, bowing as each person completed their blurb.

During the yoga sessions, the meditation aspect was what lured me into actual relaxation where I could feel the growing ball of energy between my hands. It was a unique feeling. The instructors touted physical and spiritual renewal, something which I hadn't experienced and wasn't aware I needed. Months passed and it was time to renew my program, having been offered many different training cycles, which I graciously refused, as there was little explanation as to what exactly happened in these events held sixty miles away. Much later I could see that most of the students, like me, were in some stage of vulnerability. Unlike many, I didn't buy into the need to spend many additional hours away from my work, participating in training which was designed to move one to the next level and ultimately become a Master. Aside from the constant proposals of ways for me to spend more money, the actual turnoff came while observing one of the high-level trainers, a young Anglo woman suffering from what appeared to be pneumonia, continue doing a thousand bows while she turned ashen from the effort, somehow believing that this condition would disappear from her system.

After several months it would appear I wasn't a good enough candidate for brainwashing, and I quietly walked away, having watched many students being sucked into a narrative which would eventually make headlines after a follower died on a desert outing in Arizona. The woman was forced to hike carrying a heavy backpack and not allowed to carry water with her.

In the end, there wasn't a psychic or a yogi master alive who was going to help me move forward in my life. I also knew another relationship would not accomplish that either. I was going to have to do it myself. I had now come full circle, from codependent to art dependent, or so I believed.

30 | GET SOME HELP, WHY DON'T YOU?

WAS I SUBCONSCIOUSLY LOOKING FOR another relationship? I thought not. Convinced nobody else would want me and that I was forever stuck in limbo, I was surprised when a man who hung around the same fraternal club began to flirt with me as I sat waiting for the bar to close so we could go home. He flirted as D and I were on the dance floor and I caught him looking at me as we all sat around the bar. It was subtle, but to my weakened ego, it was powerful and effective.

Have you ever felt as though you're jumping from a raging fire into yet another blaze but can't stop yourself? *Just what was it going to take for me to recognize the emotional peril I was in?* If someone was relating this exact story to me, I'd probably throw my arms up in the air and say *for Crissake', get some help!* The problem was that my subconscious task at that moment still seemed to find someone to love (or was it to love me?) Apparently, I wasn't finished attracting alcoholics.

After D and I had finally severed the fragile cord which held us together, and I was aware he was, and had been for some time, involved with one of the divorcees at the club, I began seeing this man on a regular basis. It wasn't long before we moved in together (of course). I slowly discovered I had been drawn to an individual who was more of an alcoholic than D ever aspired to be. What was it that was different? While D drank from five o'clock every evening, E began within minutes after awakening. At five in the morning from another part of the house I could hear the familiar sound of a pop-a-top coming off a can of Miller Lite beer. He consumed one beer after another: on the way to work, at work, at lunch, at coffee break, on the way home, at home, on the way to the club, at the club. *What the hell was I thinking,* is the question. It was obvious that I wasn't. Once more I had been sucked into a far bigger drama than I ever bargained for, and I reluctantly went along for the ride. I'm sure my ever-present optimism about fixing someone else played a huge part in my thinking.

Again, there was no justification for the reasons I allowed him in my life. I was obviously in need of intense psychotherapy, but it would take more than a few failed relationships to get me there. This could not have been the real me. Was I subconsciously using this man to make D jealous? I was foolish enough to believe that I could continue to frequent the same club on the arm of this man since it wasn't unusual for couples to trade partners and still be in the same establishment to dance and drink on weekends. This was a warped belief I would soon come to regret. One night as we drove into the back parking lot to attend the weekly western dance and drink fest, I noticed D had also driven up and it was my intent to ignore him. In a flash, he made a beeline for my car, proceeded to smash the passenger side window with his fist and literally pulled E out and proceeded to beat him unconscious.

I had never witnessed the brutality of one human being attacking another so violently. In total shock, I helped E back into the car and in a panic drove the six or so blocks to the hospital, where the emergency room physician declared his elbow had been broken in half and was only being held together by a strip of skin. I wondered then if the anger and violence might have well been directed at me and I could feel a wave of anxiety creeping back into my life. For a few days I played obligatory nursemaid while trying to steal a few moments in the studio. For the life of me, I couldn't get over the violence I had witnessed. It elevated my fear barometer to the maximum level.

Afraid that D might repeat the violence since we lived in the same neighborhood, we decided it might be a good idea to get away for a while, so we took a trip to Las Vegas. It was a long drive on a particularly hot day and my SUV's cooling system worked overtime to keep us comfortable. We checked into the Luxor Hotel, and I walked around, taking in the luxurious accommodations. A makeshift Nile River wound its way around the entire expanse of the hotel. It was my second trip in the past twenty years and there was now a lot more glitz and sparkly lights. Everything was bigger and better. Since we made the trip on the spur of the moment, I hardly anticipated the beating my pocketbook was going to take as we spent hours feeding the slot machines in almost every casino within walking distance of the hotel.

As we drove along the strip, a group of wedding chapels with white picket fences lined up like gingerbread houses came into view. I might have thought about remarrying at some point, but the red flags going off in my head were firmly imprinted on my mind. If we might have considered walking in the front door of any of the chapels, I would have hoped I would be struck by a bolt of lightning. But wait, he hadn't asked me; we hadn't ever discussed the subject. This was just my overactive mind rowing up shit creek without a paddle. Fortunately, the subject never came up.

For the better part of more than a year I existed in a fog of indecision regarding relationships. I was a self-employed artist during this time and devoted my days to creating art. My studio was the only place I could retreat to where life was harmonious and beautiful. It was after five o'clock each day that I recoiled back into my need for conflict and drama. E's drinking never stopped or slowed down the entire time we were together. What made me think I had to lower myself to his level to fit in? In my own way, I was working up the courage to tell him things weren't working out, but from past experiences, I knew it was going to be a difficult task for me to successfully accomplish.

One evening as I washed a load of dishes, E went downstairs with his can of Miller Lite held lovingly to his chest. My mother called in a state of despair, telling me that my father was ill and needed me to take him to the ER. As I grabbed my jacket and keys from the bedroom, I heard what sounded like a gunshot coming from the back yard. I ran out to the deck but couldn't see anything in the dark. My parents were waiting for me and I didn't know what to do, so I called my son and then 911 and explained what I thought was happening and went off to rush my father to the hospital. When I returned home several hours later, two police cars and my son were parked in the driveway. One officer who intimated he was a friend of E's family, said they weren't going to arrest him for discharging a firearm within the city limits, but that he needed to sober up. After the police left, my son told E he had caused enough turmoil in my life and that he needed to leave, for good. He looked at me with soulful eyes as I nodded in agreement, grateful to my son for having the strength to say what I couldn't.

The next day he called to beg my forgiveness, and could he come home. I stood firm with the decision to break it off permanently. I wasn't going to be guilted into reconciling. Weeks passed and for the first time in his life he checked into an alcohol rehab center which relocated him to Oklahoma City to undergo a detox program. It took more than a month before he returned to Santa Fe with embellished stories about all the things wrong at the rehab facility and his reasons for checking himself out. Although he claimed to have continued to be sober, the excuse was that his fellow alcoholics there were mostly rednecks and visibly racist toward him. I continued to resist his requests to come by and see me. During our time apart, I worked toward becoming emotionally stronger with the help of a psychologist, and I really didn't expect I would hear from him again. I had clearly stated I was not interested in resuming the relationship, if one could call it that, whether he was sober or not. Foremost in my mind was the thought that I would not have been able to face my son had I even entertained the idea of taking up where this man and I left off.

31 | SMOKE SIGNALS

THE SEVENTH OF JULY IN 1997 began like most any other workday in my studio. I was hurrying to complete carvings and paintings for the annual Spanish Market on the Plaza in Santa Fe coming up at the end of the month and was devoting every spare second I had to getting my work done. I realized I had wasted valuable time the past year being in a relationship which drained me both emotionally and physically, so I was determined to make up for that with new and beautiful creations of art. It was a relief to spend time alone and continue to work out the previously obvious problems in my life. I had continued my therapy sessions for several months and was content with my progress. Every inch forward was a milestone for me. Admitting I had spent most of my life in self-destructive behavior and denial was a difficult process, but we were working on it. Although rather dim at first, I was beginning to see the light at the end of the tunnel.

That afternoon I returned to the studio after a quick lunch and sat down at my worktable. I heard the familiar roar of a truck muffler on the street out front and moments later looked up to see E standing at the screen door. He said he had come by to pick up his belongings which were still stored in the back-bedroom closet. I pushed the screen door open and said it would be all right. Since he wasn't very conversational, I indicated he knew where his stuff was and was welcome to retrieve it himself. I turned and returned to my worktable as he walked across the threshold into the kitchen mumbling something about *don't worry, I'm not going to steal anything.* I thought that remark was a bit uncharacteristic, but I put it aside since at the time I figured he was now just a sober alcoholic. I needed to focus on what I was doing.

After fifteen minutes or so had elapsed, I began to wonder what was taking him so long to retrieve the few things in the closet. I made my way through the kitchen, down the hall to the back bedroom and found him sitting on a bench with two rifles on his lap and his duffle bag on the floor next to him. He looked startled and mumbled again that he wasn't stealing anything. He stood up from the bench, grabbed his stuff, and I followed him through the house and out the door. He stopped long enough to retrieve a gas can from the porch he said I had no need for. As he reached his truck, he hollered out, *enjoy your new life with your new boyfriend.* I shrugged that remark off knowing there was no point in trying to decipher another cryptic statement. I was done and I had to put this incident in some sort of perspective so it wouldn't remain in my mind and develop a life of its own. I assumed he was referring to the photographer down the street with whom I was collaborating on a book about women's shrines.

That evening as I watched a mystery movie on the Hallmark Channel, the phone rang and made me jump. It was E's ex-wife calling to ask if I had seen him. I said he came by earlier in the day to pick up his stuff, but I hadn't heard anything since then and didn't expect to. She explained he left some rather bizarre messages on her answering machine apologizing for everything he had ever done to hurt her, and that she wouldn't be hearing from him again. I commented that was probably a good thing, and maybe he was moving out of town. They had divorced after thirty years of marriage, and I knew she still hadn't completely cut the cord. I assured her I would call if I heard anything and settled back to watch the conclusion of the movie.

The next morning, she called again. Barely awake, I listened patiently as I wondered why she felt it necessary to bring me up to date on a man I had finally dismissed from my life without regret. She said he had been staying at his mother's house but had not been seen for a few days. As they searched through his duffel bag, they found a handwritten letter dated the previous day. He apologized to them for any problems his drinking had caused in their lives and ended the letter by asking them not to blame *me* for whatever happened. His brothers searched for him throughout the day, checking bars, hospitals, jails and casinos in the vicinity and out on the highway. His ex-wife and children were concerned that he had disappeared without leaving a trail or gone off on a drunken binge and been in an accident or arrested for DWI. The nightmare had just begun.

My phone rang a few nights later and I was exasperated from the caller ID indicating that his ex-wife was calling again. Surely there were other people she could call. I was nothing to her. I answered abruptly and immediately noticed she was almost incoherent as she related yet another chapter of the drama. She said that when one of E's brothers drove along an isolated trail in the wooded outskirts of Santa Fe County in the Buckman Road area to the west, he spotted a smoky haze in the distance. Thinking someone had ignited a forest fire, he drove toward it to investigate. About a mile down the road and off in the distance, he saw the smoke was not from a forest fire but coming from the remains of a smoldering Ford pickup truck that was eerily familiar. He contacted the Sheriff's Department and waited for them to arrive.

Inside the cab of the truck, the deputy discovered E's charred remains, and determined the cause was suicide by gunshot. The hunting rifles had been jimmy-rigged in such a way that when he pulled the trigger on the rifle pointed at himself, the movement set off the other rifle aimed at the full gasoline can which exploded on impact and ignited the truck. The police officer related to his brother it must have taken a great deal of planning for everything to happen in that order. In shock that E would come to such a terrible end, I gave her my condolences and hung up.

A few days later his mother called, and before I could offer my sympathy for her loss, she erupted in an angry tirade and said that if I hadn't broken up with her son, he would not have killed himself and she would still have him. I wanted to say that his family, her included, had abandoned him long before he died, but I held my tongue. Later I would be requested not to attend any of the services, and I'm not sure I would have anyway. Still fresh in my mind was the realization that he could have very well taken my life along with his on the day he last visited my house. I continue to wonder what he was thinking as he sat on the bench in the back bedroom, holding a rifle in his lap and taking far too long to gather his few remaining belongings. I am still haunted by that thought.

Some months later, my cleaning lady and I were rotating the mattress on my bed. Underneath one corner there was a handful of cash and checks. I looked at the date and realized this was money from a Christmas market the previous December. Had this man also stolen from me without my knowledge? There was no telling how much had been there originally since what remained was substantial.

32 | REFLECTIONS IN THE MIRROR

If you asked me why I stayed in a seventeen-year relationship which began its downward spiral almost from the very beginning, my answer would be that I believed it was meant to be. I wasn't psychoanalyzing my relationships, I just wanted to be in one. I could say I hadn't yet developed the courage to be on my own. I was the daughter of a binge drinker, and according to the statistics, I was destined to have relationships with not one, but two alcoholics, along with a man who had no room in his head for me or our children. I attracted men based only on *their* liking me, as if I had little or no input on the matter. They came into my life and I had no doubt I could fix all of them. Not only could I make them love me, but I could make them want to be with me forever.

I was never much of a drinker, but sometimes I felt I could have been. Most of the men I dated when I returned to Santa Fe drank—some socially, most to excess. Occasionally I would sip on a Grasshopper or a Brandy Alexander, drinks which were more like dessert than hard liquor, just to convince myself I could fit into this picture. I watched nearby drinkers as they progressed from first drink to last, which usually evolved over a two to three-hour period. I sat on my pedestal at the bar, wondering in the back of my head what the hell I was doing there. But I always stayed.

A bar was an unlikely place for me to be, even more so since I had learned a valuable lesson from the last block party I attended in Phoenix during my marriage to the children's father. Novice drinkers cannot consume Manhattans, followed by Screwdrivers, Piña Coladas and red wine and not pay for it dearly the next morning. After that monster hangover, I never wanted to see another drink for as long as I lived. At one point I couldn't feel my legs and spent the entire night sitting on the bathroom floor next to the tub, splashing water on my face so the rest of my body wouldn't go numb and I would die. I realized then that I could easily be an alcoholic, since I had inherited the requisite gene, courtesy of my father. I wondered why I learned that lesson so easily and yet could never learn others when it came to relationships.

None of these relationships were with physically brutal men, but most were masters of emotional manipulation. Each one had the ability to elevate or drag me down at will, with such subtlety. Unaware, I easily became an emotional hostage. I began to believe that I was unworthy of love, lucky to have *any* man in my life; that I was unattractive, overweight, worthless and incapable of surviving without a man. I spent a lot of time with frogs, hoping to turn them into princes. I jumped from lily pad to lily pad, but eventually spent a lot of time in the pond, dogpaddling in a circle just trying to stay afloat.

I traveled through life with my brain missing in action, moving three steps forward and two steps back, without a clue as to what loomed ahead and the overwhelming odds of survival. At that point I could honestly say I had never been in recovery mode because I never admitted to myself or anyone that there was a problem. Since I didn't drink, smoke or have indiscriminate sex, I was just fine. I had tried and convicted myself in the court of *flaw* and had yet to completely come to terms with everything I had experienced. But somewhere in the back of my mind, I knew I wasn't done yet. It would take a long time for me to realize that something had to change to assure my survival. I behaved much like I imagined the women in my life had behaved, my mother, grandmothers, and their mothers. It was in our DNA to stand by your man, no matter what.

It was without effort that I could put whatever spin I wanted on a relationship. In my mind I could take it from zero to sixty; from *hello* straight to *I do* and the imaginary white picket fence. I could easily fill in all the blanks. My illusion of what marriage involved was warped, to say the least. My parents' marriage was the only reference point I had, and it too was warped. I had virtually no idea what the ideal husband meant to me, nor the amount of work and dedication involved in raising children and making a marriage work. My parents stayed together through over half a century of discord, but they admittedly were victims of circumstance, of culture and tradition, and more so the times. That did not mean they didn't love each other. They just didn't know how to express their feelings. Because of their artistic endeavors, their lives changed dramatically after we all departed from the nest. It was as though their creative art increased their bond as each day they continued to work together at the kitchen table at their home on West Houghton Street. Each time I walked up their street around the corner from my house, I could hear the rhythmic tapping on the metal from their hammers. I never thought how much I would come to miss that sound.

33 | SQUARE PEGS IN ROUND HOLES

In my late fifties and not particularly interested in dating, I had a good laugh when I asked my grandson what the definition of a *cougar* was, and he simply responded that it related to older women dating younger men. I asked him if it was a good label or a bad one. (I envisioned a *Mrs. Robinson* type of woman who seduced younger men for her sexual pleasure, as in *The Graduate*, the iconic sixties movie.) He added that a cougar is a hot older woman with a great body, dressed in curve-hugging jeans and low-cut blouses. Anyway, I was about to find out that wasn't me.

My next boyfriend and I met at one of the Indian casinos down the highway which I occasionally frequented. He was a Navajo silversmith who sold his wares under the portal of the Palace of the Governors on the Santa Fe Plaza. I was fifty-eight and was later surprised to learn he was only forty, but oh well, dreamer that I was, it *could* work. After a few dates we set up housekeeping without a lot of effort on my part to convince him to move in. I was still willing to settle for *someone, anyone*; after all, this one might just be *the one.*

J2 was of average height, dark haired, a tad overweight and with old acne scars on his face, but his sweet personality made him somewhat attractive. He was totally devoted to his Navajo mother, who would periodically drop into Santa Fe unannounced, having taken a bus from Gallup, and proceed to stay at my house for a week or more. I was not aware she couldn't read, and one day handed her my recently published book on women's shrines. She smiled up at me and made no comment but thumbed through the book and he took me aside to explain. After that I had to search for other ways to entertain her on the many unscheduled visits, since most days he went to sell on the plaza.

J2 was kind and considerate, friendly and outgoing. He kept my 4Runner cleaned and serviced and every Sunday took the house apart and wet-mopped the Saltillo tile floors. It was a welcome change to have a little help keeping up the house. It also helped that he would later cover the utility bills and make some effort at being a weekend househusband, since the bulk of my time was spent in the studio.

Beyond the Chicago Bulls, the Dallas Cowboys, Super Bowl Sunday, casino gambling, one-inch steaks and BBQ ribs, by this time in my life I yearned for intellectual stimulation, something I had never experienced in past relationships. I would soon discover that this wasn't going to be available in my current relationship. Although somewhat intelligent, J2 was all about work, sports and food. We ate our way through every BBQ pit, steakhouse and pizza parlor from Texas to California. We traveled throughout the Southwest attending Indian markets and craft shows where he sold his silver jewelry, and to football stadiums to watch his favorite team. Following a trip to Los Angeles to attend the opening of the Gene Autry Museum where several of my carvings were on display, we stopped in Las Vegas. In a déjà vu sequence, we drove past the white-fenced wedding chapels lined up in a row, and if I felt a micro-stirring in my heart, I paid it no mind.

Life at home was comfortable: me in my upstairs studio, he in his downstairs studio. When we first met, I thought his being a Native American artist would serve as a common ground for a relationship because I believed artists understood each other and how their minds worked. It didn't. He was no more aware of who I really was and what I really did. Later I would say that he, like my previous relationships, would have been unable to write even a few lines about me had the occasion ever come up to do so. I still seemed to require some acknowledgement of my worth from the person with whom I was involved, at the very least an indication that what I was doing was important.

After a few short years of the somewhat platonic relationship we had settled into (hampered by my head-first plunge into late menopause), I discussed with my therapist the discomfort of continuing to live with this individual. I could not envision it ever going anywhere beyond where it was, living more like brother and sister, sharing the space but not the romance. As the year 2000 rolled around, I noticed I had slowly begun to press my inner *delete* button to start phasing him out. Deep inside I was hesitant to hurt him; he hadn't done anything wrong. I cared deeply for him. He just wasn't *the one* and probably never would be. I hated to break the news to him and began the conversation a hundred times but could never finish it. It wasn't about the kitchen, or the studio or the bedroom. It was about someone recognizing and acknowledging another person's worth and being able to carry on a stimulating conversation.

During one of our sessions, Dr. K, with his uncanny ability to cut to the chase, listened patiently as I reiterated all the reasons why I felt the relationship had become stagnant, there was not enough there to continue. We discussed my previous relationships and how each had ended, and I noticed the subtle raising of his eyebrows as I admitted that none of those men had ever spoken to me after the breakup. He was surprised and offered that although a relationship had ended, after the initial period of dismay most couples remained on speaking terms without hostility. That had not been so in my case. I could not even consider any of them friends. His advice was that I needed to approach the subject with J2, have a discussion expressing my unhappiness, acknowledge his, and set a deadline for each of us to move on. It was unfair to us both to continue living this lie. On our next visit, I explained to Dr. K I had tried several times over the preceding week, but the stress had created such a migraine that I couldn't finish the conversation. His sage advice this time was, *better a twenty-four-hour migraine than a ten-year headache.*

Often after a day of selling, J2 would return home with his mother in tow. I had to contain my surprise (and irritation), particularly when many times one or more granddaughters chirped along behind her. Although I never expressed it, I resented the interruption of my studio time, feeling obligated to entertain his family while he went off to sell his wares. As the situation escalated in my mind, I could very well see myself ten years down the line still struggling with the same decision, as history reflected that I had an easy time getting *into* relationships, but a very difficult time getting *out* of them. One evening I sat him down and told him the bitter truth about my feelings, and that I thought it was best for him to move on. We set a time frame for his departure to take place, and although he waited until the very last day to do so, he packed up and moved out quietly. A good friend of mine intimated I had broken up with the Navajo culture, not with the man. He was always going to be mother-oriented and unlike me, welcomed her impromptu and unannounced visits with open arms.

I admit I was a little surprised how short a time it took him to find another older woman with whom to start a relationship and they were still together some fifteen years later, albeit she lived in Texas but split her time in Santa Fe. A while back he shared that she had decided to break off their relationship. I would venture a guess that her reasons might have been similar to mine, but I didn't ask. He was feeling bad enough as it was. Today, we are still the best of friends.

For the next year or so I tried online dating, at the time the wave of the future, with little success. Men who made an initial connection could quickly drop off the face of the earth. One of them broke up in an email, and we hadn't officially met. Another one went through the initial process and then closed the match, citing *other* as the reason. I read somewhere that one of the drawbacks of online dating is that a person can experience a blow to their self-esteem by there being no apparent reason or explanation for someone discontinuing communication. I was open to taking a chance on this manner of meeting someone, but there was no guarantee an initial connection would last. I was pleased when someone I was hardly interested in communicated for a while and then met a woman closer to Florida and they are still together. My early apprehension about him was related to his online profile. He appeared to be a hard-core Jesus freak and in most of his photos there was a Cockatoo on his shoulder which he referred to as his first love. We surely had little in common. I ultimately decided these online sites had little to offer and would take too much effort to follow up, so I opted out.

And then the pandemic years hit, but by that time I had learned that I could be happy on my own. I had my art and my writing, and I continued to do what I did best. The isolation wasn't as harsh as it might have been, as I had always spent many hours alone in my studio each day. The most frightening part was watching the country go to hell in a handbasket over a situation that many thought could have been nipped in the bud.

34 | REPORT CARDS

It was difficult to acquire the skill set to walk away from a relationship on my own. There was always some perceived reason present to keep me in. Was it fear of being alone? Probably. Did I recognize that? Probably not. I created the roles I lived always based on the other person's needs, not mine. I provided nourishment for their bodies and souls, and gave until I had nothing left to give, just so I could feel loved. Whether I choose to believe it or not, I *am* capable of learning, changing, adapting; but sometimes it requires a great deal of repetition before I finally get it. Call it one of my flaws, call it a condition, or blame it on my ever-present stubborn streak of wanting things to work out no matter at what cost. I might even stretch it another level and say I was afraid to admit failure.

I had a strong survival instinct, and I wasn't going down with the ship. During these years I crossed bridges, burned bridges and finally learned to build them. I graded myself on a wide learning curve. As long as I was still upright when the relationship finally ended, I was all right. I lived in my own little world, marooned on my personal island, afraid of water and unable to swim to shore. In all these relationships with men, there was never a *me first* and sometimes there was me not at all. I didn't have a narcissistic bone in my body, but I probably should have developed a few. Yet, my accomplishments have been many. Alone in my studio spanning several decades I created thousands of pieces of traditional and contemporary art, all of which have sold.

In small increments during this period of my life and to better myself, I began attending classes at the two local colleges. In the mid-nineties, I was fifty years old and fascinating new facts poured out of textbooks and lectures, spurring on a curiosity for knowledge which had remained hidden through all my adult years. I worked toward and ultimately received a degree in Southwest Studies from Lesley College in Boston, thirty-seven years out of high school, followed by being awarded a prestigious Javits Fellowship to pursue my studies.

Since then, I have published well-accepted books on the historical churches, culture and saints of New Mexico, along with an early memoir about growing up in Santa Fe, and six mysteries set around Santa Fe, my most recent endeavor being a children's story book, which I wrote and illustrated. Starting in 1982, I created huge carved and painted altar screens for numerous historic churches in Northern New Mexico, all while continuing to exist in a state of dysfunction. Surely there was always a guardian angel hovering over me to make sure I emerged unscathed. I have been learning to walk alone, and by this, I mean not alongside a male companion. What was so difficult about it, I wondered, that I considered it daunting just to walk around the block by myself? Somewhere along the line I regained my own identity, coupled with the knowledge that I was a loving, caring, compassionate and intelligent individual, and that I always had been worthy of love. It became apparent that I had always existed in what something could be, not what it was.

Was I ever going to experience *forever after* or *until death do us part*. I still don't know the answer to that either, but now at eighty-one, the odds seem to be less and less. I continue to be envious of couples of any age, but more recently the mature ones, who at least on the surface appear to be content. I wonder what magic formula they used to stay together and still look lovingly at each other; or did they meet later in life after being widowed or divorced. I do not have a valid response to these questions either, but I hope answers will come.

35 | MIRACLES DO HAPPEN

REGARDLESS OF MY ON AND OFF RELATIONSHIP with the church, I have always believed in miracles. No, really. I have. Throughout the 1980s during my forties, I was plagued with episodes of asthma. They began out of nowhere one evening and I stood out on the deck of my house, hoping that the fresh air would alleviate the wheezing. An hour later I would find myself in the ER. Although this condition was thankfully not as serious as those I had observed in others, for several years it was necessary to use a rescue inhaler, with an occasional middle of the night trip to the ER when things loomed out of control. There I received IV doses of epinephrine, a drug which made my heart pound out of my chest, creating more anxiety than the attack itself.

During the 1990s I became friends with a Theatine priest from San Luis, Colorado and received several commissions to create religious art for his parish church. Father Pat was dedicated to preserving the traditional arts of New Mexico, a number of these arts which had also flourished in the San Luis Valley during the 1800s. He was a friendly and compassionate member of the clergy, born in Colorado and stationed at San Luis. On our first meeting, he ordered fifty small paintings of San Cayetano, the patron saint of his order to be distributed in an upcoming event.

The next commission was for a large altar screen for the Church of San Acacio in San Luis. Years later, he again visited my studio to discuss a project for a Theatine Seminary he was remodeling in Mexico and our friendship flourished as we planned out the project. That friendship has endured throughout the years. I have a great deal of respect for him because he nourished not only my creativity but also my soul.

When my father's health began to deteriorate, and despite having siblings, I took care of most of his needs. My sisters would drop by on weekends with prepared food, wash a few dishes or a load of clothes and visit my parents while sitting at the kitchen table. I was expected to do everything else, which included appointments, medications, shopping, evening meals and the like. At one point I was at my wit's end when Father Pat visited my studio. Observing my state of mind, he insisted I travel to San Luis and stay in the old convent which had been converted to a bed and breakfast. It was late winter, so there were plenty of vacancies. He and the nuns took care of me, fed me, and allowed me to rest and recover for several weeks. Never once did they insist I attend mass or confession. They just let me be in the peace of the beautiful San Luis Valley on the New Mexico/Colorado border. I returned home refreshed and invigorated and ready to continue helping my parents. My siblings finally realized the toll I had taken and increased their efforts to help more often.

At my next meeting with the priest, he unveiled the plans for me to design and paint an altar screen incorporating the saints from the Theatine Order which had been established in the 1700s by St. Cajetan of Thiene (San Cayetano here in New Mexico). Along with this saint, there were four other images, one of whom had not been canonized but was close to meeting the requirements for the process at the Vatican in Rome. San Juan Marinoni was credited with a miracle in Father Pat's small community, and little did I know he would be responsible for a miracle in my own life.

After I formulated the design which consisted of five large panels enclosed within a 40"x60" carved wooden frame, Father Pat mentioned that the miracle in his village attributable with others to this saint had been submitted to the Vatican for consideration of possible sainthood. One of Father's parishioners had been diagnosed with Stage IV Cancer and determined terminal by his doctors in Denver. As it is the custom of parishioners in small villages to visit the infirm and recite the rosary, on one occasion the priest brought with him a small silver case containing a relic of Marinoni's remains. On each of their visits, the priest placed the relic under the man's pillow while they prayed. The cancer had progressed to a point where he was barely able to function and the family prayed for a painless, peaceful death as the prayerful parishioners continued to visit. A few weeks later Father Pat stopped by the home, certain the man would now be close to death. He found that not only had he regained most of his strength, but his color had returned, and he was able to walk short distances. Doctors in Denver would declare there was no sign of cancer in his body. He had indeed been the recipient of a miracle.

Aware of my struggle with asthma, Father Pat suggested that perhaps I should pray to Juan Marinoni as I painted the panel depicting his image. I really doubted this would help, but I decided it wouldn't hurt either, so as I added color to this specific panel, I asked the saint to help me out here. What the heck, I was a good person and was doing my best to express my faith through my art; couldn't he possibly ask the Man upstairs if maybe the two of them could get together and rid my life of this condition? A month later, as I added the finishing touches to the nearly completed altar screen, I realized that it had been days since I had used the inhaler. I mentioned this in passing to Father Pat who assured me that indeed this saint candidate had listened to my prayers. Skeptic that I was, I thought to myself it was probably just a coincidence, although I was aware that the juniper pollen in the air at that time of year was twice the normal amount. For the next three months I used the inhaler only twice and eventually not at all. For three years following, I only used it on those occasions when allergens in the air were extreme. Father Pat gently reminded me that although the saints can perform miracles, they cannot control the environment. Fortunately, I have never had the need to renew that prescription, and I continue to be grateful that I was the recipient of an unexplainable but welcome miracle.

36 | DISSECTING THE FROGS

IS IT ANY WONDER THAT SOME WOMEN STAY in relationships long beyond the time they have clinically ended? It's tough to be on one's own, especially as a single parent. After the divorce from their father, my children and I survived on Hamburger Helper, Tater Tots and a weekly five-pound box of Booth breaded shrimp in between. World and local news stories held little importance—I was focused only on making it through that one day. I cared little about war, crime or international drama in the news. It didn't matter who was governor or president—it didn't affect my personal life.

I believe there should be a category in medicine for dating disorders. Too much or not enough, it's always been the same result. Most of my relationships ended on a sour note. Although for years I maintained a civil relationship with my children's father, I did so only for their sake. Every birthday and Christmas card filled with ten dollar bills *he* never sent were received right on time courtesy of the post office around the corner from our house, or my slipping a stamped card into the mailbox before asking one of them to retrieve the mail. It may have been deceptive in the long run, leading them to believe their father had actually remembered their special days, but it was a worthy lie. It saddened me to see the looks on their faces as they checked to see if there was a card for them mixed in with the junk mail, only to find nothing. As they entered adulthood, they formed their own opinions of their father without any prompting from me. Two of them believe he walks on water; the other not so much, and that is because he believes that respect is earned, and that you don't show up with gifts after the party is over. The love is there, of course, but he guards his heart. It stands to reason that I was bitter and angry, as most women would be, and that feeling stayed with me a very long time until I could walk away without regret because I finally realized it served no purpose.

I have to wonder how much of an influence my choice to pick a career in art has been in reshaping my life. Or had it picked me? If I had stayed married to my children's father, I'd probably have retired after spending forty years working in the legal field and returning to Santa Fe only to visit my parents each summer for the requisite two-week vacation from my job. Had I stayed married to my last husband for more than the seventeen years of that marriage, I'd probably be incapacitated or dead from the stress alone. By the time of my divorce from D in 1993, I suffered from almost every stress-related disease in the books, but I didn't realize that was the cause. I was overweight, suffered from migraine headaches, asthma attacks, arthritis, and so out of shape that I couldn't walk more than half a block without my heart racing. No doubt I suffered from undiagnosed floating anxiety, PTSD, and some form of depression. When I left him, I believed every nasty thing he had ever said to me. My self-esteem plummeted below the charts, and it would take a long time before I realized I wasn't any of those things.

In all those years of struggling to keep a relationship together, I dived into each one without a user's manual, oblivious that if they were worth pursuing, it would require effort, commitment and perseverance on both our parts. It was not enough to *hope* everything would work itself out. It was not enough to *wish* all the disenchantment away. There was no fairy godmother to wave her magic wand and make everything better, so each relationship and marriage slowly fell by the wayside having died from different forms of neglect. I lacked the knowledge and the skills, but still walked blindly into the next one, ever hopeful that somehow this one would magically work out.

For years I could identify with every country western song streaming over the radio. Some of them triggered an emotional response as soon as the melody began. Along with Willie Nelson's "Blue Eyes Crying in the Rain," and George Jones' "He Stopped Loving Her Today," every other song on the radio could have been composed about my miserable, unhappy life. I am certain I could have written my own song which would have climbed to the top of the charts. I graduated with honors from the Tammy Wynette school of Stand by your Man. As my life began to change for the better, it took a considerable amount of time to once again listen to this genre of music. Country music was not something I chose, it could not be avoided since I was married to a cowboy and it streamed from every pore of the bars and dances we attended. When I finally tuned my car radio to a country western station a few months later, "There Goes My Reason for Living" made me sit up and take notice. I allowed myself to listen and then shouted in my head: *That's no longer me*. These days, I find classical music a better vehicle to soothe my thoughts, and eighties hits to energize me.

Life had stopped being a fractured existence. The realization had finally set in that not everyone is a good person. My long-term relationship with D had turned bitter and angry, and I no longer wanted to be a part of it. I could tell that my therapist wanted to throw his hands up in frustration, but he didn't. He gently and firmly guided me through, and his words still resonate in my head. *No, Marie, your ex-husband was not a nice man, sober. He was an alcoholic who terrorized you and your children and kept all of you living in fear. And no, the father of your children was not a nice man either. He was narcissistic and emotionally unavailable. He abandoned all of you and never paid a cent of child support, forcing you to do the best you could with the limited resources you had. And no, you are not fat, ugly and worthless. You have managed to stay afloat despite incredible odds of survival. You are creative, talented and ingenious, but it isn't enough for me to tell you that. You must believe it.*

Sometimes I wondered if I stayed in my longest relationship because of the children or for my own selfish reasons. He wasn't their father, yet he provided a good living for us and perhaps I didn't want to give that up and return to the struggle of fending for myself. Drinking problem aside, I still believed he was a good man, but then again so was my father and look how we all turned out. All residents of Divorce city.

If it wasn't for a conversation I had with my son a few years ago, I would have never known how much emotional damage my children suffered all the years I stayed in that marriage and long after. Their psyches had been tormented, their spirits broken, and I had been oblivious to the stress and emotional trauma that caused it. Where was I during all this time? Was I in such a state of denial that I sacrificed my children's wellbeing so as to not be alone? Fact is, even while in a relationship, I was still alone. Every day I applaud my son for having the courage to explore his past, difficult as it must be, in order for him to leave it behind and assuage the trauma he endured during his childhood. Time and time again he has said that in spite of and because of what he went through with D, he is a better man.

I have never admitted out loud that I was guilty of contributing to not only the drama but the breakups. I have, however, learned something from each experience, albeit late. Despite my best intentions, something always eclipsed my efforts to not repeat the past, but I continued to do so. For most of my adult life I engaged in behavior which was subconsciously self-destructive, and I had so little self-esteem left that I participated in one-sided relationships. Had I been given a nickel for my thoughts, I would be a millionaire today if I hadn't relinquished ownership of my life. So, was I all right? *What was it that kept me afloat?* I realize it was my ability to immerse myself in my work. Creating art unwittingly became my salvation.

37 | ADVICE TO THE LOVELORN

Although I was always willing to give advice with such a believable air that female friends admired my ability to see through the BS, I never followed my own advice. As long as it was their BS I was dealing with, I was fine. I couldn't shovel fast enough to step out of my own. I am convinced that for most of my life I have never been *in love.* I have loved; I have loved the idea of love; but to my knowledge I have not been *in love.* I have been mostly *in need, in want.* Every magazine, newspaper article, TV program, country western song and even the Holy Bible has something to say about love. Whether you experience true love in a lifetime remains to be seen. There is a perception of love in modern society that has clouded the rose-colored glasses I always peered through. These days the idea of marriage or a committed relationship seems to strike a fearful chord deep within the average individual, many of whom are in their mid-thirties before they take a trip down the altar. They want some assurance that things will work out. I have news for them. There is none.

My ex-husband of seventeen years never spoke to me again after I finally left him the second year after our divorce. He was a bitter and angry man, and although I felt the need to remain friends, he would have nothing of it. I took advantage of every opportunity but he would cut me off at the pass and not engage in any interaction between us. I felt I needed to communicate, if only to convince myself his professed love hadn't really turned to hate. But it had. Fifteen years after we went our separate ways, he passed away, having requested some time before his death that I not attend his funeral. *What was up with these men that they thought it was necessary to preclude me from paying my final respects?* Some weeks after he passed, I stopped by Rosario Cemetery to drop off a bouquet of flowers and thank him for having at least been a semi-adequate father figure for my grandson. It was a bittersweet closure, but a closure, nonetheless.

I finally understood that his childhood traumas had molded him into a suspicious, angry, jealous, sadistic, manipulative man. Through deception, his grandmother stole him away from his mother and denied him any contact, although he would later find unopened letters from her expressing a desire to see him. Maybe he couldn't help himself. His grandmother dictated his every move, instilling a sense of entitlement and suspicion in his young mind. To put it bluntly, during our marriage he constantly accused me of screwing everyone in sight, whether associates, clients, friends, or business acquaintances. Being barred from E's funeral also precluded closure to that period of my life, knowing I would have been bombarded with dirty looks from the family. For a short time, I included him in my morning meditation. I threw in a few prayers, hopeful that through his final actions he was able to find the solace he never had on earth. One can hope both these individuals are resting in peace.

38 | FAITH, HOPE AND CHARITY

About fifteen years ago, on a wintry Sunday morning ten days before Christmas, I awoke with the intention of attending mass. Forty years since my first divorce (the only wedding ceremony in a Catholic Church), I had returned to the religion of my childhood. Unless I was under the weather, I never missed Sunday mass, Lenten or Christmas services, or funeral masses for family and friends. Each time I stood in line with others to receive Communion, I felt a bit of pride that I was able to participate in this ritual, it having long been absent from my life. During childhood, religion was not a subject we discussed at the dinner table. We were automatically born into Catholicism, period. Nuns at St. Francis Parochial School pounded into our heads that every time we committed a sin, a small black dot would appear on our hearts until there were so many that it was completely covered. We were too young to comprehend what a soul was, so a white heart was used symbolically. On a weekly basis, all the first and second grade students were herded into St. Francis Cathedral, seated as a group, then lined up to enter the confessional.

Unless one was headed for sainthood, we had little understanding of just what all this meant. We were terrified that we would be struck down by lightning, so we prepared our mental lists, reviewing what we perceived to be sins. And then, by some magical conversion in a cabinet-like confessional, we emerged cleansed of our perceived terrible misdeeds, until the next time, which we hoped to avoid by being better children. Penance usually consisted of five Hail Marys and two Our Fathers. We vowed not to lie, or steal, or curse, (most of which we never did) or anything that would sentence us to a lifetime in Hell. After two years of Catholic school education, transferring to a public school brought forth differences which confused my sister and me even more. There was no daily mass to attend, no prayers or moments of silence. No saints and guardian angels watching over us. Discipline was also different—no sharp raps on the knuckles with a wooden ruler or having our ears pulled by a cranky nun in a black habit.

Confessions were still stressful as an adult. Kneeling in a claustrophobic closet-sized wooden stall measuring some 3'x3'x8', I waited apprehensively for the penitent in the other closet-sized side to conclude their confession to the priest who sat in an equally sized middle closet with two 16"x16" screened and curtained panels on each side for the accumulation of sins to be whispered. *What was the big deal, I wondered? Where did this fear come from?* Beginning in childhood we were taught that any infraction committed would place us in a bad light and confession was necessary in order to purge these sins from the soul. In addition, it was the pointlessness of admitting your frailties to a priest who had never dated, married, or experienced much anything else due to his vows of celibacy. As I write this statement, I wait for the lightning bolt to hit my house simply because I have thought such a thing.

Sitting in that tiny box, the priest became bigger than life, ready to whip you into submission through prayer and chastisement for your sins. At least that's how I viewed it as a still-attempting-to-be-Catholic adult, so I tried to rarely require confession but usually blew it when I missed mass for no reason at all, and that was a no-no. (When I mentioned in passing to a cradle Catholic about not being able to receive Communion without first going to confession, she said it was hogwash. What did missing Sunday services have to do with anything? With the present state of the church, they were lucky anyone attended services at all.) Hogwash or not, this had been pounded into me and every other Catholic schoolmate since childhood and it was also clearly stated in the first pages of the daily mass guide in each pew, and of course I believed every word.

Over time, my faith in God and myself slowly eroded. (Which came first, the chicken or the egg?) I couldn't figure out how and why my life had gone so far afield. I know now that it was because my entire life *was* my relationships. I was so intent on making them work that I had little room for myself or anything else. Did these men bail out when the relationship turned serious, or when they realized it would never be serious, or if it was all me? Was I not beautiful enough, funny enough or intelligent enough? I certainly was willing enough to carry both of us on my shoulders. Did they chase me until I caught them because I not only desired a relationship but felt it necessary to have one?

There were times in my life when I walked away from religion. It all seemed so pointless. I wanted to remain a believer but when I considered the condition of my own life, I couldn't see what purpose it served to continue blindly trusting that which I couldn't see. This God I believed in had in recent years taken not only my parents but five of my siblings and a few of my close friends. I felt like an orphan with nobody to turn to for comfort. I yearned to belong to someone, something. My life had been a struggle and no amount of prayer seemed to change that. My state of spiritual confusion was due for a shakeup. During the mid-1960s when I lived in Phoenix and felt the need for some spiritual solace and respite from my fears and loneliness, I wandered into St. Thomas Catholic Church on Seventh Avenue. I remember sitting in a wooden pew toward the back of the church, tears gently streaming down my cheek. I sobbed quietly as those around me stood and formed a line and walked toward the altar to receive

Communion. I realized my sadness was caused by the early divorce which precluded me from participating in the church rituals I had learned as a child.

More than thirty years would elapse before I would pursue the marriage annulment process offered by the Catholic Church. After submission of countless forms with answers to hundreds of extremely personal questions involving sex, drugs and probably rock and roll, I dived in head first. The "tribunal" required two letters of support from persons who knew me during that Catholic marriage (which had lasted less than three years.) These letters would of necessity come from two of my remaining siblings. The Tribunal would ultimately determine that when I entered into the marriage, regardless of my age, I had been too immature to fully comprehend the meaning of a lifetime commitment. This was prefaced with a comment that an eye should be kept on my future relationships, whatever that meant. I assumed they were referring to my other marriages, although neither of them was through the church. And besides, were they going to follow me around to make sure I stayed on the right religious path? I resented the hierarchal attitude imposed on my request for annulment, but I stuck with it and it was eventually granted.

When I again departed from the church, my therapist at the time offered that faith was going to be the solution. What did I know about faith? What did I believe about faith? Did I even have any? I never could *let go and let God.* I didn't really believe that anyone but me could do it. By letting go that meant relinquishing control. It was difficult for me to believe that God had brought me this far and would take me all the way.

As a child, I must have lived in fear, in apprehension (a condition which seems to still hang out in the fringes of my life). The therapist and I discussed matters that were deeply embedded, only to discover that I never had a real childhood, and that's why my recollection was sparse in places. My mind was occupied with always waiting for something to happen and hoping it wouldn't;

and if and when it did, being powerless to stop it. I could pray for a solution, for a resolution, but I didn't have the faith to do that. I believe that the difference between prayer and petition is that in petition you turn over to a higher source a specific thing that you can't handle and pray for it to be taken care of and have absolute faith that it will be, and then move on. Dive into faith headfirst, wash yourself in it, embrace it, and believe it . . . and then believe it some more, even if you find yourself apprehensive about trusting that the problem will be taken care of. It was not an easy concept for me to embrace, let alone comprehend.

Try as we may, it is a virtual impossibility to control our environment and situations we may sometimes find ourselves in. So, it is in acceptance and having faith that the situation will be resolved. Petition for faith, pray for resolution. That was a hard order for me. In 1997 when my brother Bobby died at the age of sixty-four, I was angry that God didn't see fit to make him well. I believed that by praying and having copious amounts of faith, He would listen to me. When He did not, I was disappointed, disillusioned, and angry. I wondered, what purpose did faith serve then? A priest later said to me that my brother was responsible for the ultimate end of his life by his early use of drugs, alcohol and smoke. What did it matter that years before his death he had already cleaned up his life and had become a creative force following in my parents' shoes and taking their craft up yet another level? What was disappointing was that my prayerful petition hadn't been heard or even considered. I believed I was a good person, worthy of having a wish granted and when it didn't happen, it made me sad, angry, and disappointed. I stopped going to church for a long time, but eventually came to terms with my anger and returned.

But that return to religion was also short-lived. As a vulnerable human being, I could not ignore so much conflict existing in the Catholic Church related to pedophile priests and their actions being covered up by popes and bishops most Catholics admired and looked up to. Even my own family dynamics rubbed against the teachings of the church. How can you love someone who creates so much conflict in your life? Forgive, yes; accept, no. Drifting away from the church didn't come easily. It was a slow journey, like a lazy stream running through a parched desert. I needed the ritual of religion; I longed to belong. But my sensitive heart couldn't take the constant turmoil boiling over and hitting close to home. Even priests who were my friends eventually couldn't walk the path. It was not up to me to be their judge and jury.

At St. Francis Cathedral, my childhood church, I was faithful for a few years before I became disillusioned with what the church had then become. To add to that, before my brother Ricardo passed away, he intimated that as an altar boy when he was ten years old he had been inappropriately approached by a priest. He didn't go into detail but said he never returned to assist at mass and had little need for religion after that. It also galled me that a priest whom I admired, enjoyed his sermons, and who had even attended my lectures on saints and churches, was arrested for having an affair with an underage girl from his home country. I could not comprehend the duality of the man's life. We were taught to hold the Pope, bishops and priests in high esteem. Perhaps it is too much to comprehend that the church requires a caring and sensitive individual such as myself and others to set aside and ignore all the feelings and emotions brought about by the constant barrage of negative publicity and yet continue to blindly support it.

These days I occasionally stop by the cathedral and wander through the aisles, looking up at the walls on each side which house the fifteen Stations of the Cross I created for the church in 1997, and pausing in the north chapel to say a few prayers to La Conquistadora, the patroness of the church. But instead of attending church services, my practice is to do a daily morning meditation, much as my mother did, which includes a rosary and prayers to the Holy Spirit and the saints. Yes, I do still miss the ritual of the mass, but I don't have to pretend I belong there. In December of 2018, the abuse situation tragically hit close to home. The

Archdiocese of Santa Fe filed for bankruptcy because of numerous lawsuits filed against them for the actions of several priests serving in New Mexico. News coverage of the pedophile problem continues on many levels, with loyal Catholics expected to bear the burden with their weekly donations.

39 | SEARCHING FOR TRUTH

In moments of self-analysis, I still had many questions about myself. Why did I feel so unworthy? I considered myself to be a decent person, and of adequate intelligence. I often wondered if my parents, kind souls that they were, had been disappointed in me because of the choices I made. I was certain they hoped I would initially settle down for good with a nice, hardworking man who would provide for me and our imaginary flock of children. I'm also certain my mother reached for her rosary each time she learned I was in yet another relationship. In retrospect, I'm sure they just tolerated my chosen partners, and if the need arose, lambasted them in private.

They would not have understood my reasons for searching beyond the horizon. That I felt different, was different, not fully engaged in their rules of religion and culture. I had my own narrative about searching for love, one which even I didn't understand but that would take almost an entire lifetime to lead me to wholeness and stability. Perhaps if I had developed better communication skills from childhood on, things might have been different. But even as young women we were taught that men were superior, and that fact came to light each time the subject of equality came up. Men were the bread earners; women were the chief cooks and bottle washers, hardly entitled to a reasonable salary for their efforts. My older sister, then in her late seventies, told me that on one occasion our father remarked that the reason I had such difficulty with relationships was that because none of those men understood me. He saw who I was and how I was different. How insightful that was of him, and I wish he had shared that with me.

During all the years that I have been attempting to write this memoir, I believe I have grown in spades. Sometimes it was two steps forward and three steps back, but subconsciously I was learning to maneuver my way through life as a willing participant and not being hauled along for the ride by some meaningless relationship I had thrown my whole basket of eggs into. I learned that I always had a choice, and whether I made the right one or the wrong one, it was still my choice. My common-sense filter became fully operational and I use it often to make decisions based on what's right and what's wrong, and what's right for me; not based on whether another person will be angry or disappointed if I disagree, or like or love me less.

Did I regret any of my relationships? I believe the regret was that they didn't fulfill the fairy tale. Each knight was flawed. He had a chink in his armor, a nick in his sword, or maybe just rust in his joints, I don't know. I was lured by the possibilities, the potential, not the reality. I was not drawn to white collar workers or professional men because I had no training in wifery. I had never developed the social skills necessary to move between what we then perceived as social classes. I could not envision myself as the wife of a professional person, capable of entertaining guests at dinner parties, or even socializing with them. I did not have the composure, the wardrobe (or the self-esteem) to place myself in the running. I imagined blue collar life was less stiff, less demanding: sports, bars, blue jeans and t-shirts. Nothing threatening. I never had the opportunity to discover whether I would have fit in or not. Over the years I have had many affluent clients, some of whom have become good friends, and I feel comfortable interacting with them regardless of their wealth. One even assured me that I would have fit right in and probably been happy at it.

There were many times I had felt alone even when in a relationship. There was nobody to comfort me, to assure me everything would be all right. My baloney detector never seemed to function, and I was naïve enough to believe just about anything. It seems odd to consider that I spent my entire life pretending everything *was* all right—that I was able to survive pretty much anything. But was I? Not so much.

"I counted them up a while back—all the guys I'd ever dated. It surprised me that the number was so high. I always thought I was a wallflower. As I made a quick review, it dawned on me that none of them were real. Each time I had only imagined they were the one, the true love, the white knight, the elusive love I had looked for in all the wrong places. And why was it necessary to fantasize, he asked, with his PhD in hand. I don't see the reason for the need to make them something they weren't. My response was simple, neither did I. I was marinated in the pleasure of being someone I was not. Oh, don't get me wrong, there was no raving beauty here, no long-legged vixen, but enough of something to attract these erstwhile men. I don't know. They were mostly a mix of musky aftershaves, clean cut and gentlemanly. I was well versed in the fantasy of them enjoying my company, and I theirs. Ah, euphoria. Those first kisses were very special indeed. What if I never experience that feeling again?" (Excerpted from Lowrider Blues, Sunstone Press, 2009, Marie Romero Cash)

My children's father and I have become better friends over the years but shared few intimate facts about each other's lives until recent years. We discussed my writing of this memoir, and he wondered how I was able to review more than fifty years of events in my life. He laughed when I said they were tucked away in a specific storage unit in my brain and that it was time to sort through them. I took him down memory lane about when and where we met, and we talked about life since our divorce. He revealed that early in his second marriage, he discovered that the woman for whom he left me turned out to be much different than what he bargained for. Time would reflect they were ill-suited for each other and would eventually divorce after she turned into Dr. Jekyll and destroyed their relationship and the accompanying financial stability he had worked so hard to attain during their years together.

One of the most fascinating and helpful discussions we had was when I asked if he recalled whatever had prompted us to leave the art institute in Santa Fe without having planned anything out. His response was that we were young and impetuous and didn't bother to think things through. We shared a laugh as he reminded me that because at the time we ran off he was a student and ward of the government, I would probably just be getting out of Folsom Prison if the feds had caught up with us on our merry journey to the west.

Obviously on the same brain wave, our son also gave me a lot to think about as he analyzed some of the things I expressed. *Look at it this way, Mom. My dad was barely twenty-one when you had your first kid; by the time I came along, he was almost twenty-six and by then had three kids. You guys went straight from dating to playing house, the Vietnam War intervened, and he never had a chance to ever play the field and grow into a well-rounded man. You were probably his first serious and long-term relationship. Nothing personal, but he was a guy. I'm sure he was curious about whether the grass was greener on the other side. Unfortunately, we were all caught in the consequences, you included.*

So, it was never about he didn't love me; it was about he never got to know me well enough to establish a foundation for love. For so many years I believed he left because of that lack of love; that I wasn't good enough, smart enough, pretty enough. Maybe if I had asked the question even twenty years ago, I wouldn't have been able to process that answer because I still harbored some bitter feelings about his lack of support for our children and me. Now I can. I now realize that I jumped into each relationship without ever taking the time to know the person or for them to know me. Had I done that, I might have had a lot fewer relationships and saved myself a whole bunch of grief. But then again, that would have hijacked my learning process and not given me the opportunity to grow and get to where I am now.

In November of 2023, my children's father visited for a month, staying with our daughters. On Thanksgiving Day, it was the first time in fifty years that we sat at the table as a family. I do believe it was a therapeutic event for each of us, particularly for our three adult children.

40 | ART BECOMES LIFE

DURING THE 1980S AND EARLY 1990S, my creative process provided an income separate from that of my husband. My inventiveness propelled me into a wider circle where years would pass before I felt both welcome and comfortable. There were many more men in the arts than there were women. Creating traditional art was more fulfilling than any relationship I'd ever had. I was still married and the lack of quality in the marriage contributed to the imbalances in my life. While in my studio, the earth stopped its rotation. I could wander deep into myself where ideas flourished, and I could develop the ability to transfer these ideas into wood sculptures and painted religious icons. I created art from the ashes of the bridges I burned behind me.

In the 1970s when I returned to Santa Fe, I taught myself to paint retablos and carve *bultos*, the traditional art of the 19th century *Santeros* (saintmakers) of Northern New Mexico. Over the decades I carved and painted many hundreds of madonna figures, angels and saints and a whole slew of other subjects including good and bad girls of the bible and painted boxes depicting scenes of Old Testament life. At some point my creations drifted toward more contemporary figures such as Joan of Arc and a woman carving the Statue of Liberty, pushing the envelope at every opportunity. One of my earliest innovative pieces was a carving depicting the "*Onion Lady*," a story from the Brothers Karamazov. Somehow, I knew that particular narrative from the story could be converted to wood. From there on, innovation became second nature. I created large multi-level winding staircase pieces with different carved saints on each step, topped by gatherings of angels. Those were followed by a series of wheels of life with different scenes on pedestals attached to the spokes. I can proudly say that in addition to the many church commissions which remain in situ, my works are in collections of major museums, which include the Smithsonian, the Museum of International Folk Art, the Gene Autry Museum, the Colorado Fine Arts Center, the Vatican, and private collectors such as Bill O'Reilly, Joe Garagiola, Tony Hillerman, Mary Higgins Clark, and others.

Becoming a successful artist was not instantaneous. It was a series of hundreds of baby steps and false starts, followed by short strides and lunges. I can't say being an artist was ever a part of my original life plan, but it became my life, and I embraced every opportunity to create. I had never developed (or even considered) a formula for success. I would later learn that success is the ability to do what you love, without bankrupting yourself to get there. I fell into art like I fell into a relationship. I was there, art was there. We kissed and embraced and then moved in together, 'til death do us part. It was the most important commitment I had ever made.

Creating art is not much different than reciting a prayer. As I create, I am on a different plane. I am not thinking about a trip to the grocery store, bills to pay, a car to service, a phone call to make. Art is where I go to refill my glass, to partake of the creative expressions which emanate from a higher source than myself. The Holy Spirit is the source of *Me*, a spiritual energy that infuses my every movement with creativity. To fashion a slab of wood into an image of a saint or a contemporary figure is a process that I learned through trial and error. I was not taught to carve and paint. I learned it on my own. As I researched and documented the historic art in New Mexican churches and published books related to the subject, my inner database increased. I look back at some of my early pieces and I can see the progression over a forty-eight-year period. It is truly amazing to me. I started out on a small scale, painting in acrylics and then graduated to watercolor, as these were closer to the colors used by the original Santeros in the mid-eighteenth century. There was a specific palette developed by these early artists: indigo, Cochineal red, ochre, green, light blues, blacks and browns, all created from natural pigments, plants and flowers. After a while I found this to be too tedious of a process and chose to continue with watercolors.

My first major project was for San Juan Nepomuceno Church in El Rito, a twenty-two-foot-high altar screen with large panels depicting the patron saints of the village. As I continued my career, I was called upon to create large works of religious art for several historic churches in northern New Mexico and southern Colorado. The impact of these commissions never swelled my head or my bankbook. I worked within the priest's budget and I was honored to create the art. All these monumental pieces still stand in the churches for which they were created, at El Rito, Ojo Caliente, Espanola, Arroyo Seco, San Luis and Pueblo in Colorado, Santa Maria de La Paz and St. Francis Cathedral Basilica in Santa Fe. I also created art for the Archbishop of Santa Fe's private chapel in Albuquerque and a screen for the Catholic Center there, which is the backdrop for the Sunday Mass on a local TV channel.

I don't believe I consciously aimed the direction of my life toward creative endeavors. It could be that it was meant to be. I'm often asked where I get so many ideas. Truthfully, they just come to me. I never considered that over the span of years, every piece of art I had crafted would be sitting in someone's home, a museum, or church. Each painting or sculpture I created gave me faith that I would be able to survive, and contrary to all the negative messages I had received over the years, I could make something of myself. I have learned that we rarely recognize in ourselves what another person sees. On a regular basis I am stopped by women who say, "Oh my God, you are so famous, I love your work." And men who say, "My wife and I have collected several of your pieces, and we love them." These genuine remarks have a strong impact, as they reinforce that I am doing what I need to be doing, and perhaps should continue for as long as I am blessed to do so.

In 2009, when my brother Jimmy was diagnosed with Stage 4 rectal cancer, without hesitation I promised him I would walk by his side and see him through the journey. Throughout the months of endless appointments, scans, radiation and chemotherapy, I found that there weren't enough hours in the day to focus on generating a body of art, since carving was a bit time consuming and required the concentration I didn't have at the time. My art then took a side road down unfamiliar territory. Never having painted with acrylics, I began a series of 24x36" canvases and worked on them when I returned home after addressing my brother's needs for the day. Painting provided the calm I needed after being bombarded with emotions I stifled in his presence. He was tough and expected me to be tough, but I needed an outlet to release those pent-up feelings.

Most days when I had a free moment, I would paint on these canvases for hours at a time. I could say each stroke magically appeared. Every dab of paint I applied was with little effort on my part, and when the painting reached a certain point, it was complete. Each of these abstract angels had a crown, a heart, and she was wrapped in voluminous wings. The backgrounds were filled with symbols gleaned from sources that popped into my mind, hieroglyphs, Native American, East Coast, Aborigine, Alaskan, extra-terrestrial and any other images that chose to show up at the tip of my brush.

By the time my brother's illness had reached the point of no return, I had amassed a series of over thirty canvases, each different and unique, and each representing the love and spirituality the closeness to him provided. The number of painted canvases has continued to grow over the years and the subject has remained the same. Angels that remind me of his presence.

41 | LIFE CHANGING COMMISSIONS

BEGINNING IN THE 1760S, A SMALL GROUP of mostly-untrained artists created religious paintings and carvings to decorate the barren walls of the adobe churches, mentored by the Franciscan priests governing Northern New Mexico. In the early 1970s, I began to follow in the footsteps of these early Santeros by establishing myself as a saint maker, a career which would follow me for almost half a century. That early religious art had existed mostly unrecognized until the Archbishop of Santa Fe expressed the need to incorporate the art into the most important church in the diocese, St. Francis Cathedral. He developed a committee to explore the possibilities and they proceeded to set the wheels in motion.

The committee developed a list of artists and invited us to dinner at the archbishop's home in Albuquerque. In the weeks following, the same artists met with the committee, and we were asked to provide a portfolio and our thoughts about such an undertaking. At the end of the meeting, we were requested to each submit a painted panel of the 13th Station of the Cross and informed that the artist chosen would receive a commission to paint all fourteen panels. I was both excited and apprehensive at the prospect. To my credit, I had painted those large altar screens for several historic churches but had never attempted to paint Stations of the Cross, as the examples in the churches I had documented consisted primarily of framed Currier & Ives color prints and etchings supplied to churches when the railroad established a route to New Mexico. There were no painted images by those early artists available as examples.

I set about preparing to paint my submission, and on several visits to the church I realized that the complex combinations of color made the task additionally difficult. Stained glass windows throughout the nave contained their own color scheme, and the completed paintings would be placed between these windows. The rector of the church indicated to me that the colors in my proposed panel should not clash with the windows. Right on schedule, the five of us delivered our panels. When I saw the other entries leaning up against the wall in the conference room, it was the first time I realized how serious the competition was. Each of the artists had submitted their finest work. Not any one of these panels was like the others. The subject matter was the same but there were five different renditions for the committee to consider.

After several weeks elapsed, I was convinced my submission had not been chosen for the project and set about preparing for an annual market coming up in July of that year. In the middle of May I received a letter from Archbishop Michael Sheehan filled with sincere congratulations informing me that I was the artist chosen for the commission to paint the fourteen Stations of the Cross. (The following year a donor would commission me to paint the 15th Station, expressing that a panel of the Ascension would complete Christ's journey.)

I set about looking for examples on which to base the fourteen paintings. I explored books, drawings, paintings and actual stations *in situ*, but I kept going back to those I had seen during the daily mass on EWTN, the Alabama Catholic channel. I needed clearer images and contacted the station and spoke to one of the nuns about perhaps obtaining photos. I was told I could purchase a packet from the gift shop, but that same day Mother Angelica, the prioress of the order told them to send them on to me. In May I received the packet of photographs of mosaic tile Stations which I initially thought were paintings. Alabama was an unlikely place to find something I might use as a basis for a project here in Santa Fe. I studied them for the positions of the figures, not the colors, since they were composed primarily of red and white.

I continued to search through the Vatican collections, German, Lithuanian, Spanish art, and every source I could access. A photographer friend, Siegfried Halus, gave me a packet of postcards of carved relief Stations from a church in the UK which took my breath away. These would assist in interpreting the three times Jesus fell, stations three, seven and nine. Ultimately, I used a combination of six different examples to come up with the images I would sketch. Robert Montoya, the carpenter chosen for the project, cut the panels so they would be uniform and delivered them to my studio. Early on, I became aware that realism had not been part of my self-taught training. I could only draw simple hands, not realistic hands. It took a great deal of research and practice to eventually be satisfied with the positioning of the hands on the many figures involved. To accomplish this, I sketched my daughter Audrey's hands multiple times, having her hold slabs of wood in her hands to emulate a cross.

In the fall of that year, I took a break to travel to Cambridge, Massachusetts to complete the requirements of my BA in Southwest Studies. I was away from home for seventeen days, tying up what I hoped would be a major part of my education. While on campus, I found myself tired, anxious to be home, closer to my roots and family. I struggled to attend endless meetings, interaction with endless individuals and continuous research. I longed to return to my project and express myself through my work. Yes, I experienced happy and quiet moments, but also moments of unexplainable despair, impatience, loneliness . . . a deep desire to resume the journey. During that time in Boston, I felt stifled and stagnated, as though the air there was not filled with the creative surges I experienced at home. I knew that an explosion of creativity would occur once I boarded Amtrak for the journey home.

I was elated to be in my studio, which was now filled with thirteen gessoed panels, some on easels and some against the walls. I worked every day for months, using holy water as a vehicle for the pigments, feverishly assessing my work with a critical eye. When I began the 12th station, The Crucifixion, I decided to honor my family by incorporating as part of the design the names of my ancestors beginning with my parents, followed by the names of my siblings and their families, and my children and grandchildren. Mary's veil is decorated with a prayer for me and for everyone who enters the cathedral. By this, I asked for prayers for the Pope, Archbishop Sheehan and the priests of St. Francis Cathedral. I wrote the prayer in Spanish, and although it is not visible from the aisles, I know it is there. When all the panels met with my approval, I applied varnish to the surface, waited a few days and then loaded them up and delivered them to the carpenter to be placed in the frames he had constructed. Once he delivered them to the church, they were stored until preparations could be made for installation.

Following the Ash Wednesday evening Mass at St. Francis Cathedral on February 12, 1997, Archbishop Sheehan blessed each of the new stations with holy water and incense. He then led the congregation through the church, meditating on each station. As he welcomed the new additions to the cathedral, he stated that the inclusion of "santero" style Stations of the Cross honored the traditional religious art of New Mexico. He also emphasized that Catholic devotion to the stations was an important part of New Mexico's religious tradition and were central to the spirituality of New Mexicans. I was present with my children and the carpenter who had created the frames. I took all the pomp and ceremony in stride, shaking the hands of many friends and parishioners when the celebration was concluded.

The full impact of the commission had not hit me until October 4 of that year. The Feast of St. Francis was a First Friday, and I had occasion to attend mass. I walked through the church to the chapel of La Conquistadora as I often did after services. I lit four votive candles (a habit of mine), one each for my parents, children, and myself. I lingered for a moment, contemplating the current events of my life. I walked back across the church to see how the Stations were holding up, how the light reflected on them. As I stood near the 13th Station, the panel which I had submitted for the competition, I noticed a woman standing next to the pews gazing up with her eyes closed and realized she was deep in prayer. It hit me then . . . the fact that someone, anyone, was actually praying before or to something that I had created. This was the most awe-filled moment I had ever experienced. That someone would find peace and comfort in my work was far more important than whether it was "pretty," or well done. This body of work was to be, is to be, hanging in this church for all time . . . long after my death . . . long after there is any memory left of me. It entered my mind that I was chosen for that moment, and it had always been my destiny.

42 | ON BECOMING A WORDSMITH

LIKE MANY TEENAGED GIRLS GROWING UP in the 1950s, I read Nancy Drew Mysteries. There were few books in our house, perhaps a couple of encyclopedias pushed on my parents by an aggressive door to door salesman, and not much else. My father enjoyed reading, but mostly about history. In the mid-nineties, becoming an author came about because of my curious nature. I wanted to know more about the individuals who created the polychromed and painted wood carvings of saints found in the historic churches of Northern New Mexico referred to as *bultos*. My interest was fueled through a grant from the National Endowment for the Arts in 1987. I was able to conduct a survey of the traditional art in these churches with local photographer, Jack Parsons. We found many examples *in situ* which had remained unseen by the general public. We photographed and documented hundreds of unique examples of each Santero's work, along with many by theretofore unknown artists. These examples allowed me to closely compare the painting and carving styles of these individuals. An artistic eye was instrumental in observing the unique stylistic differences. I set about writing a book that on the one hand would be scholarly, and on the other hand easily understood by the lay person who desired basic information on the subject.

The Santos book was followed by books on churches, women's altar shrines, a memoir about growing up in Santa Fe, a Pueblo Revolt romance, and a children's book. Becoming a mystery writer came about by accident. Tony Hillerman, New Mexico's most revered author, passed away in 2008 and in the spring of the following year, his daughter's foundation increased the annual Hillerman prize substantially for an unpublished manuscript written by a new author. Although I had never explored fiction or even read a mystery, my son encouraged me to submit a manuscript, adding that he was confident it was something I could accomplish. I began reading mysteries by a multitude of writers. Anita's husband and my brother Pat provided hundreds of suggestions on popular authors. At last, I completed and submitted a manuscript, waiting anxiously for word. Unfortunately, that year the foundation did not declare a winner.

So, long story short, I found myself with a 50,000-word novel relegated to a drive on my computer. Good fortune arrived through an encounter with an individual who was writing a book on traditional arts which included my parents' accomplishments. During an interview, I casually mentioned my dilemma and he put me in touch with a publisher that was accepting new authors. Since that first encounter, they have published my series of Jemimah Hodge mysteries set around the Santa Fe area, the last of which I declared to be the final one. The entire experience was an unexpected adventure, which I cherish to this day.

When I ponder about the subject of writing, I do believe that it became a vehicle to express myself, to become a storyteller. Many of my books contain little bits of myself, events I have experienced, and real-life characters drawn from those who have entered my life in one way or another.

43 | CULTURE CLASH

In families of Spanish origins there is a fail-safe element involving the eldest child that, when adhered to, can create unimagined repercussions. In the early decades of the 20th century, the practice of the oldest child in essence overseeing matters relating to the deceased parent(s) was uncontested. This was primarily because families were large and the eldest would have been presumed to be the most mature and thereby capable of not only holding the family together but also in making sound decisions related to inheritance.

On the day of my father's demise, presumably because my parents might have mentioned this practice in passing over the years, and before rigor mortis had even set in, my sister Anita decided the task of caring for my now-widowed mother had fallen on her shoulders. That very day, she took Mother to her home, set up a nice bedroom and a table with a few of her tin stamping tools, and consequently my mother never returned to the house she had known for the previous 57 years. (It was an odd, spur-of-the-moment decision, one about which my sister would express her regrets years later.) Of course, we attended my father's funeral as a family, and probated the estate, and life went on for the rest of us, traveling back and forth to Eldorado, a community southeast of Santa Fe, to visit our confused but smiling shell of a mother.

After several months elapsed, the burden became greater than my sister had anticipated, and our family met to discuss the situation. One brother's house was too far away, another's home had a sunken living room, and my house had a steep winding staircase. We agreed that our sister-in-law, Bobby's widow, would take over Mother's care. This lasted for several months until the issue of money reared its head, with her stating that others who did home care were paid far in excess of the Social Security check we provided, which we believed was sufficient. Anita's daughter then stepped up as the caretaker, and then sometime down the road she was taken to our sister Rosalie's home in Albuquerque. My mother must have felt like a ping-pong ball, going from one family home to another, her mental condition deteriorating as time passed, and after several years with Rosalie and her husband, where she received excellent care, she was transferred to an Alzheimer's facility. Mother would eventually pass away there, never again recalling the life she had led and the family who loved her. This insidious disease robbed her of the knowledge and memory of all that she had been as a mother and an artist. I was saddened that there was no family at her side but was told she died peacefully in the middle of the night in 2002 at the age of ninety-three.

My next visit would have been the following day, and I had already gathered mementos to take with me, as was my usual practice. Each time I visited I would bring along family photo albums and sit on the couch with her, turning the pages and commenting on the pictures, none of which she recognized, even those of herself. One time I showed her a photo of a beautiful colcha stitch cross she had made, where my father had surrounded the stitchery in decorated tin. It was one of their signature pieces, one which had appeared in an article in New Mexico Magazine and again on the cover of the Santa Fean Magazine. She looked at the photo, and her eyes twinkled as she smiled and said, "Did you make that?"

We all had fond memories of our mother. Throughout my teen years, my sister and I sat with her in the kitchen listening to radio dramas (comparable to later television soap operas), notably *The Romance of Helen Trent* and *Our Gal Sunday*. I imagine now those were a precursor for young girls to be caught up in the idea of the knight in shining armor. Even my father rooted for Helen to find romance.

Some years earlier in 1998, when my father became aware of his imminent death, I stood by his bed chatting away to fill the void. For some years he had suffered from mysterious ailments caused by his many years of working in Los Alamos where he had been exposed to various elements such as Plutonium. He raised his hand and said to me that he had always loved my mother. I motioned her over from the kitchen and told him that he should be saying these words to her. I'm sure she had always longed to hear these words, even though his actions throughout their marriage disproved them. Days later, his caretaker called to say my father's health was rapidly failing. I rushed over and sat by his side. No matter how difficult I had perceived my upbringing to be, I realized he was about to depart this earth and I would never see him again. I held his hand and assured him that he had been a good father, an incredible artist, and that he was loved by us all. It didn't matter whether he could hear me or not. He passed quietly. I gathered the available family and when they arrived, we recited prayers around him. I wondered later if I should have been more understanding of his life, but I hadn't yet had enough psychotherapy to do that. Weeks later I spent an hour at my therapist's office, pounding on pillows and screaming at the top of my lungs to release all the anger and sadness I had endured. I wasn't sure if it would work or not, but I participated anyway.

At both my parents' funeral services, every pew in the cathedral was filled. My father had been baptized, confirmed and made his Holy Communion there. At their funerals, it was humbling to discover that so many people knew and respected our parents.

The church was filled with relatives, friends, neighbors, artists, museum staff, local dignitaries, collectors and admirers of their work. A standing-room-only event.

44 | PASSING THE TORCH

My parents' creativity filtered down to all their offspring. All seven of us inherited or developed an ability to create art in one form or another. My brother Emilio was a master metalsmith, able to fashion large sculptures from copper sheets, do bronze casting and other forms of art. Bobby, Jimmy and later Pat followed the tinsmithing tradition; Rosalie was an accomplished stitchery artist like my mother; Anita was a carver/painter of saints, a Santera, her works being in great demand during her lifetime and even after her passing. The two of us had parallel careers, using similar methods but stylistically different.

It never occurred to me that my process in creating art is in any way special or different than that of other artists, but I guess it is. I strive to inject a bit of humor and whimsy into each piece. I want to delight the viewer, whether they make a purchase or not. I want them to walk away smiling. My method of creation is more complex than just carving and painting. It began as an attempt to carry on the traditional arts which had been introduced to Northern New Mexico in the mid-18th century. This became more difficult, as after a while, there were many artists now attempting to do the same. My work then began to lean toward more contemporary representations, and many awards later, I discovered that was a niche where I fit comfortably.

My parents had accomplished extraordinary things in their later lives. They were considered national treasures, honored as a couple by the National Endowment for the Arts for their skills as master craftsmen. In 1987 my mother took her first airplane trip at the age of seventy-seven to attend the award ceremony in Washington, D.C., which my father could not attend. They were presented with certificate signed by President Reagan, of which they were equally proud. They received the Masters Award for the many years they participated in the Spanish Market, along with being honored by both the State of New Mexico and the City of Santa Fe, all through which they remained humble.

As artists, my siblings and I were also variously honored, with many kudos being heaped on Anita. Jimmy was chosen by the City of Santa Fe to create the massive tin border surrounding the upper part of the southside library exterior; Bobby opened a gift shop at the LaFonda Hotel featuring his award-winning creations in tin; our family was featured in many magazines and newspaper articles. I, too, reaped my share of awards, garnering many blue ribbons and the Masters Award over the many years in Market, being chosen to receive the Mayor's Award in 2019, being the first United States artist chosen to participate in the International Folk Art Market, honored by Women in the Arts, and a number of other occasions.

I must admit that I envied that my sister Anita had fared far better than I had in marketing her art. That is not to say that I wasn't successful, but due to my existing emotional traits, I sometimes lived in a "never enough" state of mind. She chose to retire shortly after the height of her career, wanting to focus on her husband's health and her own medical issues. I was with her in a noisy cubicle in the ER when she passed away after having suffered a massive blood clot. Lying quietly on the hospital bed, she was still beautiful, with perfectly formed eyebrows and porcelain skin. I held her hand and spoke to her until her last breath. My daughter Audrey and I found ourselves alone with her in that room, watching and listening to the beeps and hums of the machines to which she was attached. A nurse came in and administered a shot through the IV, and moments later my eldest sister, an amazing artist, departed from this world, leaving behind a legacy for many to enjoy for years to come.

During the next decade, I would witness the demise of five of my remaining siblings. The loss of my parents had left me feeling like an orphan, and with the subsequent passing of my siblings, a state of aloneness I had never experienced set in. I no longer had brothers to lean on for help, or a sister to call and hash over the trials and tribulations of my life. Although my remaining sister still lived in Albuquerque, she had begun to drift into memory loss, but I continue to this day to make it a point to not forget her birthday.

45 | PERSONAL SHRINES AND HOME ALTARS

THE TRADITION OF PERSONAL HOME FAMILY SHRINES was one I held dear to my heart. For an exhibit of my personal shrine in 2007 at the Museum of International Folk Art in Santa Fe, I wrote about the reasons why shrines had endured in our family and neighborhood.

There are never enough saints, there are never too many saints. There's always room for one more. My shrine served as a reminder of many things. Everything on it was important. For some things I have forgotten the reason, for many I can remember only too well.

People leave us, but they leave things behind. Small, inconsequential bric-a-brac that sometimes holds their souls inside. My mother's tattered old silk coin purse still has a bit of change in it. A small cardboard gift box still holds some of the things she had with her at the "home," not our "home" but "the home." A copper bracelet and a broken string of Mardi Gras beads from one of the celebrations there. The last hand-crafted tin crown my brother Bobby made for me before he died. He didn't want to go to the hospital until he had finished it. I didn't put it on the piece it was intended for because I would have never seen it again. It sat against his framed picture, a reminder of the great craftsman that he was and that he was taken away all too soon. The domed tin box he created the summer before came to me quite by accident. I was in Colorado Springs for a market sponsored by the Taylor Museum, and Chris Jones, the gift shop manager came by my table to visit. He said he had something special he thought I needed to have. It was a beautifully hand-crafted tin box which Bobby had sold him the previous summer. I traded a grouping of my retablos for it . . . the best bargain I ever made.

There were multiple rosaries on my shrine, some randomly collected, some gathered over the years. Dead people's rosaries, just as precious as when they were alive. Some sparkled in the sunlight, some glowed in the darkness of night. Some belonged to my mother, Senaida, one to her sister, my Tia Brigida, and the other to their cousin Belle. Others were precious metals dulled from many years of use. But all had been used for prayer. I never realized how many beautiful rosaries there must be. I used to think they were all the same, until I began to collect them and realized that many lovely rosaries have been created by fine craftsmen, using precious glass beads and fine silver chain and some more primitive, strung from wood beads.

Over the years, my shrine consisted of various personal items from Anthony, the grandson I raised. When his friend from Santa Fe Prep was killed in an accident on Valentine's Day, it was a very sad time for him and his schoolmates. At the funeral the family distributed small teddy bears to the students, which Anthony placed on the shrine along with his photo. These served as a reminder that sometimes life is cut short and we don't know the reason. Every time the roses my son, Gregory brought me began to wilt, I would turn them upside down to dry and then stick them in another vase, so the memory and the smell remained. Family mementos took up much of my shrine. A fragile crown made of waxed beads was worn by my grandmother, Anastasia, at her wedding in 1909. She was twenty years old when she married Albert Romero. It had been worn by her mother, Ciprianita Trujillo, in the 1880s. I donated the crown and its glassed wood box to the New Mexico

History Museum. A few years after the Museum exhibition, my shrine traveled in a van with me to Miami for an exhibition at FSU.

There was never much of my own work on the shrine, as it wasn't a shrine to me, and yet it took on a life of its own over the years, dismantled and distributed when I sold my house, but since it was photographed for my book on shrines, it remains a distinct memory there and in my heart.

46 | SWIMMING TO SHORE

WHY IS IT THAT SOME INDIVIDUALS ARE DESTINED to retrieve the brass ring and others spend their lives just reaching for it? Why do a select few have the Midas touch when it comes to success, finances, employment, relationships and other life events, and who or what determines that? Is there such a thing as a success gene and at the other end of the spectrum a loser gene? Is it all a mindset? Are we programmed by our surroundings, i.e., the influence of parents, their values, how they felt about money and success, immersion in the culture, the placement of women in society?

In my generation, young women were taught to believe that men were the bread earners, the wives stayed at home to raise the children, cook the meals and keep the house neat and tidy. I never excelled at those written-in-stone requirements, but I am a damned good artist and I hope I am an example for young (and older) women that the clue to success is to follow their hearts and not buy into someone else's idea of what they should be doing.

If I learned anything at all, it was that an individual carries their home in their heart. For a long time, I was not aware of that fact. Wherever I was, I always yearned to be "home." Little did I know that I was always there, or it was always within me. Alone with my thoughts, I yearned for some connection to family. I would pick up the phone and talk for as long as I could just to hear my own voice. You can't touch the cheek of the voice on the other end; you can't embrace it or look into its eyes, but these conversations were the only mode I needed, if only for that moment.

Why had I not been able to enjoy a sunset or a sunrise? Why did I not like snow? Why did I never lay on the grass and look up at the stars? Our front and back yards were mostly hard-packed dirt but would have been ideal for communing with nature. I have yet to do that as an adult, but as I age, I have noticed that clouds actually have edges and are not just big puffs of cotton candy floating through the sky, propelled by gentle breezes.

Many stories still remain, some embellished to hide the pain; some told tongue-in-cheek; and others related perhaps with as much truth as I could muster up at the time. I am no longer the child-woman I once was. My age has not sunk in as a number. Exactly what is age supposed to look like when one feels younger than that number?

I did not know I would have been able to reach into my heart for everything I searched for . . . love, companionship, approval, advice, and answers to the many questions that flooded my brain: why am I here, who am I, where am I going, where do I need to be? It is obvious to me that I need to enjoy every sunset and sunrise, and even relish the winter snow. I need to lay on the grass and look up at the stars, or marvel at the whiteness of clouds and the blueness of the New Mexico sky. And probably I need to keep asking questions, even if only of myself.

Unless one is a genius equipped with great abilities to read their own mind, the answers can be fairly elusive. They are all out in plain sight but obscured by one's own tunnel vision. We all have the innate ability to pursue our goals, no matter how little we believe in ourselves. Inner strength resides deep within, and it will rise to the surface when most needed. There is not a speck of light at the end of the tunnel—there is a canyon of dazzling golden brilliance waiting to envelop a soul. The sound of music is not distant. It is in the heart, waiting to be heard. Listen . . .

47 | EPILOGUE

As 2023 winds down, I spend time either at my computer, working on words, or in my studio, wondering what to create next. Mortality is on my mind a lot these days, as I have friends of the same age who have passed on. I have not only said out loud but have prayed that I would like to be able to create significant art for many more years to come, and I am hopeful that this prayer will come to pass.

One of Kenny Rogers' greatest hits was *The Gambler,* where the words have meaning to many, including myself, that of knowing when to hold them and knowing when to fold them. I plan on holding all my cards to my chest, since I believe I still have many hands to play, many paragraphs to write, many saints to paint and carve, and a whole lot of gratitude to express. That is what I will ante up when the game restarts.

MARIE ROMERO CASH was born in Santa Fe, New Mexico where she has resided for most of her life. She is a mystery writer, author of the Jemimah Hodge Series, along with numerous books on the religious art and culture of New Mexico, on which she has lectured throughout the Southwest. In addition, she is also an award-winning artist, and has been featured in numerous book and magazine articles about her traditional painted and sculptural works which are in many museum and private collections throughout the United States and abroad. In 2019, she received the Mayor's Award for her contributions to the arts, culture, and community of Santa Fe. Her dog, Milly, a Border collie mix, has accompanied her for many years on their life journey.

www.ingramcontent.com/pod-product-compliance
Lightning Source LLC
Chambersburg PA
CBHW011549070526
44585CB00023B/2520
* 9 7 8 1 6 8 4 9 2 1 6 5 2 *